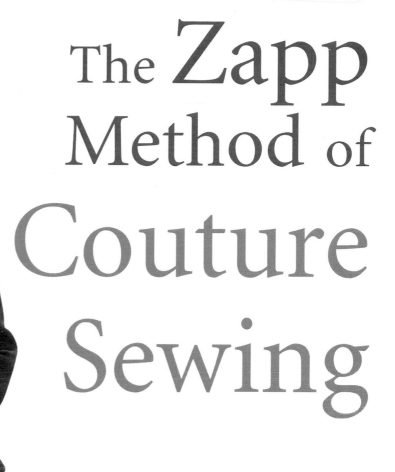

The Zapp Method of Couture Sewing

Anna Zapp

Published by

krause publications

An F+W Publications Company

700 East State Street • Iola, WI 54990-0001
715-445-2214 • 888-457-2873
www.krause.com

Our toll-free number to place an order or obtain
a free catalog is (800) 258-0929.

Library of Congress Catalog Number: 2003115536

ISBN: 0-87349-681-7

Designed by Jon Stein
Edited by Barbara Case

Printed in the United States of America

The following trademarked or registered product or company names appear in this book:
Amazing Designs®, Armo® Weft, Cactus Punch™, Eddie Bauer®, French Fuse™, Fusi-Knit,
Fusible Acro, Stacy's® Shape Flex®, Suit Maker Fusible, Sure Foot System™, Textured Weft,
Tilt'able™, Whisper Weft, Veriform

Cover photo by Mellisa K. Mahoney

To Ray, My Husband

Thank you for your never-ending support, encouragement, patience, and love. Without you, I could not have written this book.

Thank you for all the dinners you cooked for us when I was too tired.

Thank you for helping me know when it was time to call it a day.

Thank you for encouraging me to take some time off and play golf.

Thank you for being you, my love, my friend, my partner.

Acknowledgments

I want to first thank Krause Publications for having faith in my knowledge, ability to write, photograph, and illustrate my methods. It has been a great journey and I have loved the work and working with everyone at Krause. My editor, Barbara Case, has been a constant help and has been there for me at my every turn. Krause has made it possible for me to share my methods with all the wonderful sewers and designers who have the love of creating custom clothing.

Thanks to all of my wonderful clients and friends who gave me the license to design and create for them for 25 years. Without you all, the methods would not have been born.

I also want to thank the following people and companies who were so generous with their knowledge, support, and encouragement.

Elfriede Gamow, owner of Elfriede's Fine Fabrics, Susan Igou, owner of Studio Bernina in Boulder, and Jeanine Garrity. They contributed information and beautiful fabrics to the book and have always been there for me through all of my custom sewing years and my business ventures.

Sandra Betzina for sharing information with me about her pattern fit while stuck on the highway in a snowstorm on our way to Denver.

Martha Pullen, who loved my welt pockets so much that she had me do them on her show. She has also been a great advisor to me.

Terry Siemsen, my good friend and owner of Thimbles, Etc., who loved the methods I taught her and relentlessly insisted that I needed to write a book.

Clotilde, who has been a good friend and a loyal supporter of my endless endeavors in the sewing industry. She has always been willing to share her knowledge and experience.

Jane Garrison of Bernina of America, who sent me a machine to use so fast it made my head spin.

Bill and Lindee Goodall of Cactus Punch, for giving me the artist license to design disks for them (Signature #21 and Signature #55), and for their constant support and friendship while I wrote the book.

Amazing Designs, who also let me design embroidery disks and express my love of graphic art.

Gail Brown, who always took time to answer my e-mails in the midst of co-writing her own book, *Simply Napkins*.

Diane D'lea Denholm of D'leas Fabric and Button Studio in Denver, who contributed the beautiful wool for the suit featured in the projects and who has been a great supporter of my classes, patterns, and other artistic endeavors.

Laura Taylor, Assistant Editor of *Sew News*, who continues to have faith in my knowledge and ability to write for the magazine, and is a friend and personal supporter of my career.

Christine Shock, my Adobe graphics guru, who was my Illustrator and Photoshop instructor and helped me with my illustrations when I got stuck.

Steve and Karen Baldwin of Sew Vac of Boulder, who were kind enough to loan me brand new Pfaff, Baby Lock, and Elna machines. They have been great supporters of my classes in Boulder.

Bob and Karen Juenemann of Make It Sew and Quiltequipt, who were so helpful with the Janome that I was able to take a much needed day off!

Paul Arnold from AAA Sewing and Vacuum Centers for providing me with Viking and Brother sewing machines to use and who is always willing and eager to help with anything I need to promote the cause of sewing.

Rennie Zapp, my dear friend (and ex-husband), who was sure the second western shirt wouldn't take me 18 hours to make.

Rosie Cabas of The Cotangent, a store long gone in Boulder, who taught me discipline and the importance of perfection when sewing. If I hadn't met Rosie in 1971, my life would have definitely taken a different road.

A special thanks to all of my wonderful girlfriends and my two sweet stepdaughters, who were always there for me even though I disappeared for weeks or more at a time.

Lastly, I have to thank my buddies Lukie and Alli, my two black cats. Lukie made sure I took lots of breaks to play fetch with him. He watched the printer, making sure it was printing while Alli guarded my manuscript, acting as a big furry paperweight. They were sure to let me know when it was supper time, time to quit for the day.

Introduction

During the 25 years I have spent sewing – mostly alone in my studio – I never dreamed that the funny little ways I had of doing things would be of value to anyone but me. I am happy to be able to share my methods with you and hope they are helpful and will increase your joy of sewing beautiful garments in less time and with less frustration.

The satisfaction and sense of achievement you experience when you finish and wear a garment you've made for yourself (or someone else) is indescribable. I realize that sewing garments has taken a back seat to embroidery and quilting and I believe part of the reason is that fitting can be difficult and ready-to-wear clothes are more affordable these days. However, ready-to-wear can't match the detail, quality, and fit of a custom-made garment.

This book addresses the aspects of garment sewing that often cause difficulty for student sewers in my classes. I offer commonsense techniques for pattern fitting, construction, and tailoring. It has taken me many years to develop these methods. Once I had a good background in traditional tailoring methods, and after years of altering designer ready-to-wear and manufacturing my own line of designer western shirts, I was able to develop my own methods of couture sewing.

The methods presented in this book evolved from my need to sew garments for clients in an expedient and professional manner, and to be able to easily alter the pieces when my client's measurements changed. Had I not developed these methods, I wouldn't have been able to make a living doing couture sewing.

You will learn how to take your measurements and use them to tailor any pattern as well as how to copy your favorite pair of pants. I don't instruct you to do a lot of basting but if you feel the need to baste any areas, please baste. I don't tell you when to use a press cloth, but you should use a press cloth when necessary. I don't always cut out the points of notches, I sometimes make ¼" clips. If clipping makes you nervous, please cut the notches however you like.

You will find construction methods for six garments – a pair of pants, a shirt, a western shirt, a lined vest, a camisole, and a tailored jacket. If you want to improvise on any of these methods, just know that there is more than one way to skin a cat. If another way works for you, please use it. You will be able to duplicate and apply the methods to any style of garment that has the same parts.

My general philosophy is to get it done, put it on, and wear it out! I hope you agree!

Contents

Tools of the Trade

In the chapters that follow you will learn methods of construction for six garments. My approach to supplies and equipment is that you should use what you are comfortable with. There are many tools available that will achieve the same result so I leave the choice up to the individual artist (such as shears vs. rotary cutting, etc.). There are many superior sewing machines on the market and they all have fine features. When constructing garments, you will need a machine with a zipper foot, a blind hem feature, and a zigzag stitch. Sergers also are very helpful when finishing seams, but there are many ways to finish a seam.

I have had many studios in my lifetime – some quite large and some very small. Because I got tired of searching for the tool I needed, I found that having a set of tools at each workstation made my work go faster. This doesn't mean that I have three pairs of 8" cutting shears at the ironing board and the sewing machine, but I do have the appropriate size scissors at each place.

Below is a list of the tools I keep at each work area. Depending on your preference and the type of work you are doing, you might alter this list, but this is what works for me.

Cutting Table

I always have shelves built above my cutting table to accommodate all my tools and keep them in easy reach.

- 8" bent handle cutting shears and/or rotary cutter
- 10" pinking shears
- magnetic pincushion
- hem gauge
- markers – white pencil, chalk, water-soluble marking pen, disappearing marking pen, pencil
- tape measure
- 18" clear ruler
- 36" ruler
- curved ruler and/or French curve
- fabric weights
- regular tape and removable tape
- pattern paper (under the cutting table)
- interfacings (under the cutting table)
- seam ripper

Sewing Machine

- 3" or 4" trimmers
- 5" or 6" trimmers
- magnetic pincushion
- hem gauge
- markers – white pencil, water-soluble marking pen, disappearing marking pen
- point turner/small Phillips head screwdriver
- tweezers
- machine brush (a coffee brush is great)
- machine oil
- seam ripper
- machine accessories
- thread (in arm's reach)
- Tilt'able and Sure Foot System (optional, but very nice)

Ironing Board

I have a shelf near my ironing board to keep these tools handy. In my current studio, I put corner shelves at the end of my ironing board. A shelf mounted behind the ironing board at the same height would also be useful.

- 7" bent handle cutting shears
- 4" trimming scissors
- magnetic pincushion
- hem gauge
- tape measure
- markers – white pencil, water-soluble marker, disappearing marker
- press cloth
- nonstick press cloth
- spray water bottle
- lint roller
- fusible straight tape and/or twill tape
- pressing mitt
- pressing ham
- sleeve board
- turning tool
- iron
- seam ripper

Chapter 1

Customize Any Pattern to Fit Your Shape

No matter how much you love to sew, you probably find that getting the right fit can be frustrating. Many times you might spend as much time fitting the garment as you do sewing it (and the fitting is much less enjoyable). I have garments I've tried on more times during the fitting than I have worn after they were finished!

Your shape is unique and you can learn to alter any pattern to fit it. You may not get an absolutely perfect fit the first time, but the fit will be much closer than if you just cut the pattern on the size line that matches your measurements. To simply buy a pattern and expect it to fit because it supposedly matches your measurements is like shooting in the dark.

The fitting method in this chapter works for any garment and any pattern with the exception of pants. (See Chapter 2 to copy your favorite pair of pants.) The Zapp method of adjusting a pattern involves measuring your body at specific places, then measuring the pattern pieces at those same specific places. You will take your measurements, determine the amount of ease you like, and customize the pattern. Next you'll cut out the garment, baste it, and fit it. Finally, you'll transfer any alterations you make during the fitting to the pattern so that the next time you use that pattern, you can just sew and go.

> ### Anna's Tip
> **Measure, measure, measure, then cut, baste, and fit.**

This is an exercise in engineering and it's really fun to watch the pattern take your shape. After you have customized a few patterns this way, you will become quite proficient at it and will see why it is imperative to measure the pattern *before* you cut. And trust me, you will want do this every time you buy a new pattern.

In simple terms, you will find the locations of *your* fullness (not where the patternmaker put it), determine the amount of ease you like in that garment, and adjust the pattern accordingly. You will work with total circumference measurements, using either the finished amount that includes the seam allowances or drawing the pattern shape and adding seam allowances.

Step 1 – Take Your Measurements

You can take your measurements while you are fully dressed if your clothes are not too bulky. Measuring while wearing clothes may give you a slightly larger measurement but it will be a safe one. I always take my client's measurements while they are fully dressed. If you prefer, you can take your measurements while wearing only your undergarments.

Anna's Tip

Always round up when taking a measurement. I call this "safe sewing!"

Measuring is a fun exercise to do with a sewing partner. The basic measurement points are shown in the illustrations. If you have special problems areas (as we all do), you may want to add more measurement points. If you are asymmetrical, use the larger/longer measurement and make alterations to the smaller/shorter side when fitting your garment. If you are extremely asymmetrical, you may want to make two front pattern pieces and two back pattern pieces.

You may not need or use all of these measurements, but they are here for you if you need them. Add any measurements you think will be helpful. Make copies of the Measurement Chart (pages 10 to 13) and complete one for every pattern.

Measurement Chart

The measurements are numbered in a logical order for working from head to toe on a body without missing any places. Some are on the front view and some are on the back view.

Front

1. Neck _____
(total circumference of neck at base)

1a. Front neckline _____
(shoulder seam to shoulder seam along front base of neck)

1b. Back neckline _____
(shoulder seam to shoulder seam along back base of neck)

2. Neck to sleeve cap _____
(base of neck to shoulder bone)

3. Shoulder to shoulder across front _____
(shoulder bone to shoulder bone)

4. Front upper chest _____
(5" down from hollow of neck; straight across chest from sleeve seam to sleeve seam)

5. Front waist length _____
(mid-shoulder to waist over fullest part of bust)

6. Center front waist _____
(hollow of neck to waist)

7. High waist _____
(3" above waistline)

8. Waist _____
(total, measured sitting down)

8a. Across front waist _____
(side seam to side seam)

8b. Across back waist _____
(side seam to side seam)

9. Bust-point depth _____
(mid-shoulder to point of bust)

10. Bust _____
(around fullest point)

10a. Bust-point to bust-point _____
(distance between bust-points)

10b. Across front at bust line _____
(side seam to side seam)

10c. Across back at bust line _____
(side seam to side seam)

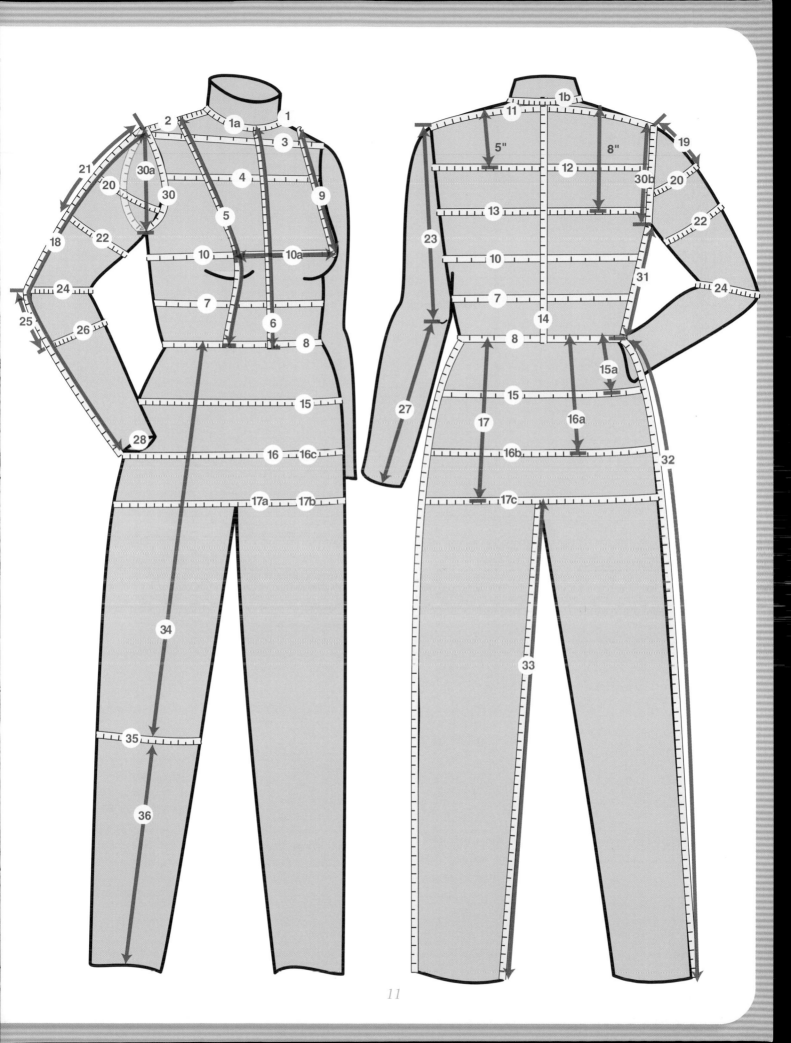

Back

11. Shoulder bone to shoulder bone across back _____

(shoulder bone to shoulder bone; across back from sleeve seam to sleeve seam)

12. Upper back _____
(5" down from base of neck; across back from sleeve seam to sleeve seam)

13. Middle back _____
(8" down from base of neck; across back from sleeve seam to sleeve seam)

14. Center back waist length _____
(base of neck to waistline)

Hips and Thighs

15. Full high hip _____
(circumference)

15a. High hip depth _____
(distance from waistline to fullest part)

15b. High hip across front _____
(side seam to side seam)

15c. High hip across back _____
(side seam to side seam)

16. Full hip _____
(circumference)

16a. Full hip depth _____
(from waistline to fullest part)

16b. Full hip across back _____
(side seam to side seam)

16c. Full hip across front _____
(side seam to side seam)

17. Full thigh depth _____
(from waistline to fullest part)

17a. Total thigh _____
(circumference)

17b. Full thigh across front _____
(side seam to side seam)

17c. Full thigh across back _____
(side seam to side seam)

Armscye, Sleeves, Cuffs

18. Sleeve length _____
(shoulder bone to wrist, with arm slightly bent)

19. Upper arm depth at fullest point _____
(distance from shoulder to widest part, usually 3" to 5" down from shoulder bone)

20. Upper arm width _____
(front sleeve seam to back sleeve seam)

21. Bicep depth at fullest point _____
(distance from shoulder to widest part)

22. Bicep circumference _____

23. Shoulder to elbow _____

24. Elbow circumference _____
(bent at right angle)

25. Elbow to fullest part of forearm _____

26. Forearm circumference _____

27. Elbow to wrist _____

28. Wrist circumference _____

29. Upper part of hand _____
(circumference, not pictured)

30. Armscye _____
(circumference completely around armhole)

30a. Armpit depth front _____
(hold ruler under arm and measure)

30b. Armpit depth back _____

31. Bodice side seam length _____

Pants

Measure your best-fitting pair.

32. Pants side seam length
(waistline to floor)
_____

32a. Right side seam length
_____

32b. Left side seam length
_____

33. Inseam
_____

34. Waist to knee
_____

35. Knee circumference
(with knee bent)
_____

36. Knee to ankle
_____

37. Ankle circumference
(not pictured)
_____

38. Foot width
(Point toe, center tape measure on heel, measure around ankle.)
_____

39. Crotch depth
(Sitting down, measure from waistline to chair seat, letting tape measure follow curve of hip. To double-check, subtract inseam length from side seam length.)
_____

40. Crotch length
(With tape measure at front waistline, keep tape close to body and take it through legs, ending at back waistline.)
_____

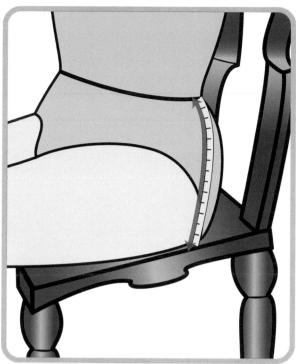

Measure your crotch depth while you're sitting down, taking the tape measure over the curve of your hips.

Jacket, Blouse, Skirt, and Dress Lengths

Not pictured.

41. Jacket length
(base of neck at center back to finished hemline)
_____

42. Blouse length front
(base of neck at center front to finished hemline)
_____

43. Blouse length back
(base of neck at center back to finished hemline)
_____

44. Front skirt length
(waistline center to hemline)
_____

45. Skirt side seam length
_____

46. Full length dress
(base of neck to floor)
_____

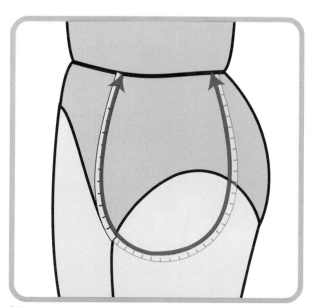

Measure the total crotch length.

Step 2 – Choose a Pattern

The good news is that you can customize any pattern from any company using this method. Buying the correct pattern size can be confusing because pattern sizes don't correspond to ready-to-wear sizes.

Choose the pattern size by the bust measurement that matches your actual bust measurement. If your bust measurement falls between two sizes, consider your shoulder width, the style of the garment, and the description of the fit of the garment. If you have wide shoulders, buy the larger size. If you have narrower shoulders, buy the smaller size. The waist and hips can be altered more easily than the shoulder, armscye, and sleeve.

Anna's Tip

If you are between size groups, consider the fit description, garment style, and your build. If the fit is described as close-fitting, choose the larger group of sizes. If it is a loose-fitting or semi-fitted design, choose the smaller group of sizes.

Patternmakers group three or four sizes in one envelope, which is a great advantage when personalizing your pattern. These multiple-size patterns provide a larger canvas to work with and give guidelines for reference. Since few people wear the same size on the top as on the bottom, it is good to have multiple sizes of each pattern piece.

There are two types of patterns on the market – traditional patterns (Simplicity, Vogue, Butterick, McCalls, etc.) and Sandra Betzina's Today's Fit patterns that are made from a different pattern block (shape) than traditional patterns. The shape of Today's Fit patterns mirrors the shape of ready-to-wear garments. They are labeled in lettered groups that relate to sizes X-S through X-L instead of numbers.

Below is a comparison chart of traditional pattern measurements and Today's Fit pattern measurements. The pattern measurements are color coded in each size category. By using this chart, you can compare the measurements of traditional patterns to the same measurement on Today's Fit patterns.

As you look at these measurements, remember that ease is not reflected in the numbers. The actual finished measurement of the garment will be larger because ease is added to the pattern.

Traditional Patterns

	XS	Small		Medium		Large		XL		XXL
Sizes	6	8	10	12	14	16	18	20	22	24
Bust	30½"	31½"	32½"	34"	36"	38"	40"	42"	44"	46"
Waist	23"	24"	25"	26½"	28"	30"	32"	34"	37"	39"
Hips	32½"	33½"	34"	36"	38"	40"	42"	44"	46"	48"

Today's Fit Patterns

	XS		Small		Medium	Large		XL		
Sizes	A	B	C	D	E	F	G	H	I	J
Bust	32"	34"	36"	38"	40½"	43"	46"	49"	52"	55"
Waist	26½"	28½"	30½"	32½"	35"	37½"	41½"	44½"	47½"	50½"
Hips	34½"	36½"	38½"	40½"	42½"	45"	48"	51"	54"	57"

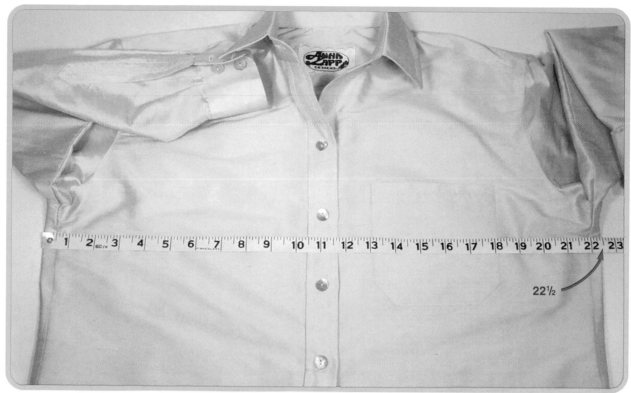

Method 1. Measure the garment laying flat on the cutting table.

Step 3 – Determine Your Ease

Ease is the magic key to getting the right fit. It is the difference between your body measurement and the measurement of the finished garment, not including the seam allowances. The measurements printed on the pattern envelope give the actual body measurement the pattern is supposed to fit, not the finished garment measurement. Ease is built into every pattern, but the amount depends on the style, design, suggested fabric, and intended fit of the garment. The description of the garment (close-fitting, semi-fitted, loose-fitting, etc.) gives you an idea about the amount of ease in the pattern, but nowhere will you find the actual number of inches allowed for ease on the pattern envelope.

Many patterns print the finished garment measurements on the pattern piece at the target bust line, target hip line, and other areas that may be important (always check these measurements). For example, a close-fitting garment will have about 2" of ease, meaning that if your bust measures 40", the finished garment will actually measure 42". A much looser-fitting garment might have 10" of ease or more. As you can imagine, ease dramatically changes the way a garment fits.

Ease can be distributed evenly on the pattern pieces, or if you are fuller across the front or back, you may want to give more ease in the larger area.

There are three ways to find the amount of ease you like.

Method 1

Find a garment that fits the way you like. Lay the garment on the cutting table and smooth it out until it lays perfectly flat. Measure across the front at the bust, waist, and hip areas from side to side (or fold to fold) and double this amount. The front of the blouse in the photo measures 22½". This tells you that the finished blouse is 45" in circumference (2 x 22½"). Hypothetically, someone with a bust measurement of 38" would have ease of 7" and this would be a loose-fitting blouse.

Method 2

Using a garment that fits, measure the finished width of the garment from closure to closure (button to buttonhole) at the bust, waist, and hip areas. Subtract your body measurements from the finished garment measurements to find the amount of ease in the garment.

> ### *A*_{*Z*} *Anna's Tip*
> **The amount of ease in a garment is critical to the fit!**

Method 3. Try on the garment and pin-fit it to your body to find the amount of ease.

Anna's Tip

To find the amount of ease using the pinch method, multiply the amount you pinched on one layer by four (because you have four pieces – two fronts and two backs). If you pinned the garment in three places, multiply by six.

Method 3

Wearing the garment, simultaneously pinch and pin it at the side seams until the fabric touches your body. Try to pinch equal amounts on each side. Take the garment off and measure how much you pinned.

For example, if you can pinch ¾" on both side seams (at any point) simultaneously, you have 3" ease in that garment at that location. If you can pinch 1" on both sides, you have 4" of ease. In the photo, I pinned ¾" on both sides at the bust line, waistline, and hip line. This means there is 3" ease (4 x ¾"), for a fairly close-fitting but comfortable blouse.

You may find that you prefer different amounts of ease in different places. The Ease Chart below details the total amount of ease you like in each location (bust, hips, waistline, upper arm, etc.).

After determining the amount of ease you like, fill out the Ease Chart and keep it on hand for measuring future patterns.

Ease Chart

Note: Add any other areas applicable to you or the specific garment.

Garment/Pattern # _____

	Your Measurement	+	Ease	=	Total Finished Garment	+	Seam Allowances	=	Total w/Seam Allowances
Bust	_____		_____		_____		_____		_____
High waist	_____		_____		_____		_____		_____
Waist	_____		_____		_____		_____		_____
High hip	_____		_____		_____		_____		_____
Hip	_____		_____		_____		_____		_____
Thigh	_____		_____		_____		_____		_____
Knee	_____		_____		_____		_____		_____
Upper arm	_____		_____		_____		_____		_____
Bicep	_____		_____		_____		_____		_____
Elbow	_____		_____		_____		_____		_____
Forearm	_____		_____		_____		_____		_____
Cuff	_____		_____		_____		_____		_____

Step 4 – Find the Amount of Ease Built Into the Pattern

After buying a pattern, you need to find out how much ease has been built into the fit of the pattern. The description of the garment will give you some indication of the amount of ease, but not the actual amount. At this point, the amount of ease in the pattern has nothing to do with your measurements.

To find out how much ease is built into the pattern, subtract the body measurement (bust/hip) printed on the back of the pattern envelope from the finished measurement of the garment at the bust/hip of that size. (If the finished measurements of the garment are not printed on the pattern, measure the pattern to find the finished amount.)

Example: Size 16 Jacket Pattern

Pattern's actual measurement

of finished garment at bust line	44¾"
Bust measurement printed on back of pattern	- 38"
Amount of ease built into pattern at bust line	6¾"

Anna's Tip

Defining the correct locations of your fullness and how it is distributed is the crux of customizing your pattern. By using this method, the pattern will start to look just like you!

Again, the locations of the fullest part of the bust, waistline, full hip, etc., may or may not be in the right place for you. The shape of the pattern may or may not be right for you, but you are going to fix that!

Step 5 – Prepare the Pattern

Most patterns give only cutting lines, so if you want to see the seamlines you will probably have to mark them yourself. If you change the width of the seam allowances in any places, note the seam allowance change on the pattern in those places (side seams, sleeve seams, etc.).

1 Cut out the pattern pieces, leaving as wide a border as possible around each pattern piece.

2 Press each pattern piece.

3 Place your completed Measurement Chart, the Ease Chart for that garment, and the mannequin drawing in plain view.

4 Lay the front and back pattern pieces on the cutting table, next to each other with the notches across from each other.

Step 6 – Measure and Mark the Pattern

My good friend and client Patty let me use her measurements as an example. Patty has a bust measurement of 38" and an average shoulder width. The bust measurement listed on the back of a size 16 pattern envelope is 38" so I bought her a size 12-14-16 pattern. (Patty was mortified when I showed her the pattern size!)

Patty chose Vogue pattern #2076, a jacket described on the package as loose-fitting. Even though the pattern states that the garment is loose-fitting, you can change the amount of ease to get the fit you want. However, I don't recommend trying to change a loose-fitting pattern into a fitted pattern. If you like a fairly close-fitting jacket, you will need approximately 4" of ease throughout the entire body of the jacket. I don't know the amount of ease allowed in all loose-fitting patterns, but this particular pattern gave 6¾" of ease in the bust and 4½" in the hip area, in all three sizes.

Refer to the illustrations on page 11 and the Measurement Chart on pages 10 to 13 to measure your body. Measure and mark twice. For the first measuring, make light preliminary pencil marks on the pattern. Then go back and carefully check each measurement, make any changes, and finalize your marks with darker pencil or pen. Then cut out your garment. (There's a good reason carpenters have adopted the "measure twice, cut once" philosophy.)

1 Neck circumference – #1, #1a, and #1b, if applicable. For 1a, measure around the front of the neck from shoulder line to shoulder line. Repeat around the back of the neck. If your shoulder line is more forward than the pattern, add the correct amount to the back of the pattern at the shoulder line. Reduce the front shoulder line the same amount, thus shifting the shoulder seam forward.

2 Neck to sleeve cap – #2. On the pattern shoulder line, start measuring on the size line that matches or is the closest to your bust measurement. In this example, the bust measurement is the size 16, or 38". The size line you start with may or may not be the one you ultimately use, but it is the best place to start measuring.

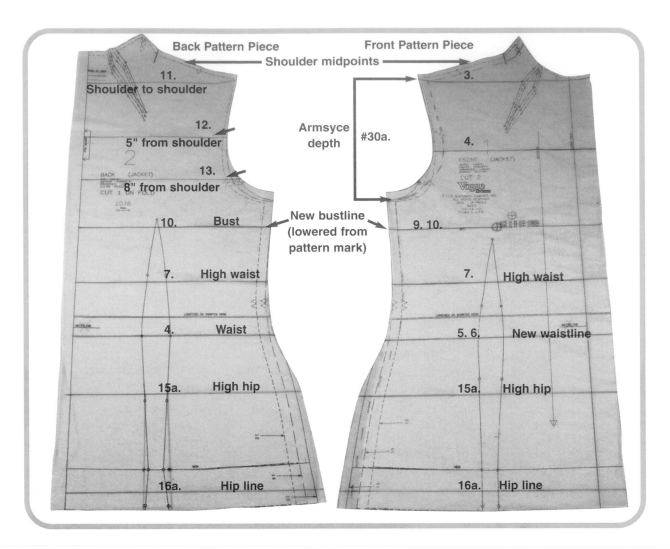

Back Pattern Piece · **Front Pattern Piece**

Shoulder midpoints

11. Shoulder to shoulder

12. 5" from shoulder

13. 8" from shoulder

Armsyce depth · #30a.

3.

4.

10. Bust

New bustline (lowered from pattern mark)

9. 10.

7. High waist

7. High waist

4. Waist

5. 6. New waistline

15a. High hip

15a. High hip

16a. Hip line

16a. Hip line

3 Compare your shoulder-to-shoulder front and back width measurements – #3 and #11 – to the shoulder-to-shoulder widths on the pattern (again starting with the size matching your bust size on the pattern). Mark the seamline and the cutting line on both the front and back pieces. If the front and back size lines don't match, average the two or go with the longer shoulder size. (Most patternmakers intend some ease across the back shoulder seam.)

In my example, when using the neck-to-cap and shoulder-to-shoulder measurements, the cutting line fell exactly on the size 14, not the size 16 (which matches the bust measurement on the pattern). This is where I put my first pencil marks.

4 After determining the correct size for the shoulder seam, measure down from that shoulder seamline and draw horizontal lines across the pattern in the following places on the front, back, and sleeve pieces. (These lines tell you the locations of your full bust, real waistline, full hip, and other places where you will measure the pattern for the right fit.)

a. Front Pattern Piece

Measure down from the shoulder seamline at the midpoint and draw horizontal lines in these places:

- 5" down from your shoulder midpoint – #4
- Armsyce depth (no need for a full horizontal line, just a mark) – #30a
- Full bust-point depth – #9 and #10 (also fullest part of bust)
- Waistline depth – #5 and #6
- 3" above waistline – #7 (You have to find your waistline before you can draw this line!)

Note: You will measure the widths and circumferences in later steps.

b. Back Pattern Piece

Measure down from the shoulder seamline at the midpoint and draw horizontal lines in the following places:

- Shoulder point to point – #11
- 5" down from the mid-shoulder – #12

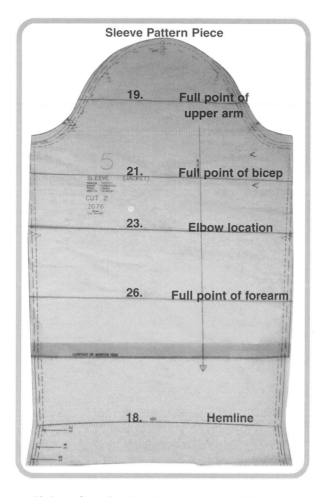

Sleeve Pattern Piece

19. **Full point of upper arm**

21. **Full point of bicep**

23. **Elbow location**

26. **Full point of forearm**

18. **Hemline**

- 8" down from the shoulder midpoint – #13
- Full bust line – #10 (same as on the front)
- Center back waistline length – #14 (from the base of the neck)
- High waist fullness – #7 (should be level with the front high waist fullness)
- High hip depth – #15a (measure at the side seam and extend the line across the back piece). Extend to the front piece at the same level.
- Full hip depth – #16a (measure in the back and extend the line to the front piece)
- Full thigh depth – #17a (measure where the full thigh can be easily seen and extend the line to the front piece)

c. Sleeve Pattern Piece

Draw horizontal lines across the sleeve pattern piece by measuring down from the shoulder bone at the following places:

- Upper arm fullness depth (from the shoulder bone) – #19
- Bicep fullest point – #21
- Shoulder to elbow – #23
- Fullest forearm point – #26
- Sleeve length – #18

5 **Choosing the center line.** If the front pattern has a center line for each size, decide which center line is best to use. Refer to your Ease Chart and look at the finished measurements printed on the pattern paper at the bust line (the total circumference at that location). Whether or not the finished amount is printed on the pattern piece, measure across the horizontal bust placement line, front and back, to get the total finished measurement. This determines the size that most closely matches you, including your ease amount.

Mark the bust-point placement (#10a) by halving the total distance from point to point, then measuring that distance from the center line. Compare the shoulder seamline size and the bust line seamline size and choose the appropriate center line size. If they are not the same, use the center line that matches the bust line size. Use that center line when measuring all other places on the pattern.

Note: *After you've made your preliminary marks, you may decide to change the center line.*

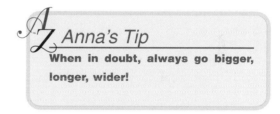

Anna's Tip

When in doubt, always go bigger, longer, wider!

Make the first markings with small pencil marks to give you an idea of the lines you will draw and cut on. If you find discrepancies in lengths or widths between seams that will be joined together, go with the longer or wider measurement. You can always reduce them.

6 **Marking the seamlines.** Measurements #3 and #11 are already measured and marked so measure and mark #4, #12, and #13 to define the front and back sleeve seamline on the pattern pieces. Since you've drawn your horizontal measuring lines to identify your fullness locations, measure the pattern at these places and mark the seamlines and cutting lines. Remember that you are working with measurements for the total finished garment (which includes the ease). That's why you lay all your pattern pieces – no matter how many – next to each other to get the total finished amounts in the correct places.

Begin with your full bust-point (the shoulder-to-shoulder and armhole seams are already marked). Use your Ease Chart and work with the "Total Finished Garment" number. If your pattern shows the finished garment measurement, choose the size that is closest to your finished garment number (which includes the ease). Begin measuring the pattern from seamline to seamline at the location of your fullest bust-point. Work with total circumference amounts first. If you have a

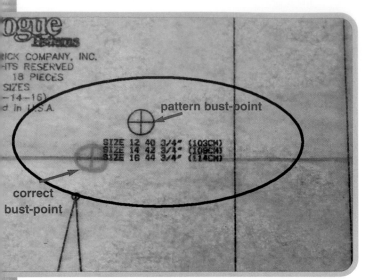

The finished measurements printed on the pattern at the bust line. (Double-check!)

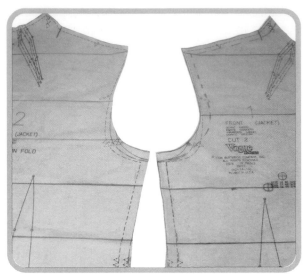

Match the new armscye shape of the front pattern piece to the back.

large discrepancy between the front and back widths of your body, balance the pattern after you determine the appropriate seamlines. First define the seamlines, then add or subtract to meet your individual fullness.

In Patty's case, the bust measurement is 38". Using 4" of ease for a close-fitting jacket, the finished garment at the bust line is 42". This finished amount falls on the size 14. (Even though Patty's bust measurement matches size 16, the size 16 finished garment measures 44¾".) The bust line point (#9) is slightly less than the pattern but since the size 14 finished bust measurement is closest to the actual finished bust line measurement, I began measuring on the size 14 seamline on Patty's full bust line.

Using your Ease Chart, measure across the pattern on all the remaining horizontal lines you have drawn, using the same method as on the bust measurement.

Refer to your Measurement Chart and measure the armscye depth front and back, then compare it to the pattern armscye depth. Look at the style of the pat-

tern and note where the armhole depth is to determine if that is the look you want. You might prefer the armhole closer to or farther from your body. If so, you can raise or lower the armhole. In Patty's jacket, I raised the armhole ⅝".

If you make changes to the armhole shape, remember to adjust the matching sleeve seam. If you change the shape of the armhole on the body of the garment, remember to adjust the sleeve seam in all the places you adjusted the body. If you decreased the armhole across the front, add that amount back at the sleeve in the same place.

Measure and mark the sleeve pattern piece using the applicable measurements, #18 through #30. When marking the size line for the sleeve cap, use the same size line as the shoulder line.

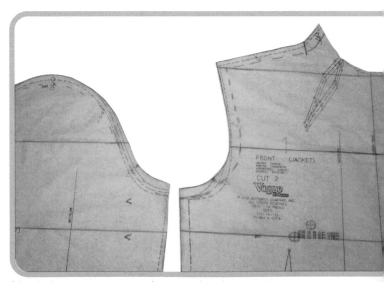

Match the new armscye shape to the sleeve pattern.

Measure the length of the finished garment and compare it to the pattern. Lengthen or shorten it to your liking.

Anna's Tip

All armholes should be somewhat lower than your armpit, but the lower they are, the less movement you will have. Cutting the armhole higher is never a problem because you can always lower it later. Lowering it too much is when the real trouble starts, because it's very difficult to correct.

7 There are several ways to adjust patterns to fit. I prefer measuring and drawing the correct lines if possible, but all the methods listed below are acceptable. I have used all of these methods (sometimes all on the same pattern).

- Fold the pattern on the lines designated for lengthening or shortening the pattern.
- Cut the pattern horizontally and add the necessary amount by inserting pattern paper.
- Redraw the seamline and the cutting line.
- Slash and pivot, or slash and spread.

8 Double-check your preliminary marks. When you are confident that the light pencil marks are in the right places, make more visible marks and draw the cutting lines. Make sure all the adjoining seams are the same length and width, keeping in mind that some seams (especially the shoulder seam) may need a bit of ease.

9 Pin and cut out your revised pattern from the trial fabric, or if you feel confident, cut your fashion fabric and proceed.

Step 7 – Cut, Baste, Fit, and Transfer Changes to the Pattern

1 Baste, don't sew, your trial garment.

Anna's Tip

It's tempting to skip the basting step, but don't do it! Most of the time you will want to make changes and it is much easier to take out basting stitches.

2 Check the fit and note any areas you think need to be adjusted. Check to see that the shoulders fall in the correct place, the amount of fullness in the body is correct, and the sleeve length and garment lengths are correct.

3 When you are happy with the fit, transfer all the alterations you made to the garment back to the pattern. For example, if you took in the side seams ½", take ½" off the side seams of the pattern. If you shortened the sleeves, take that amount off the sleeve length. The next time you make this pattern, it should be a good fit. It may need a little tweaking on the second sewing, but by the third time, it will be perfect (assuming you don't change the fabric type dramatically). You now have a master pattern of this garment and can make style changes to it if you like.

Review the Pattern Example

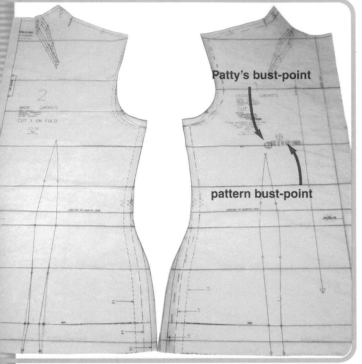

Patty's bust-point

pattern bust-point

The new pattern shape and cutting lines to match the measurements, plus the ease.

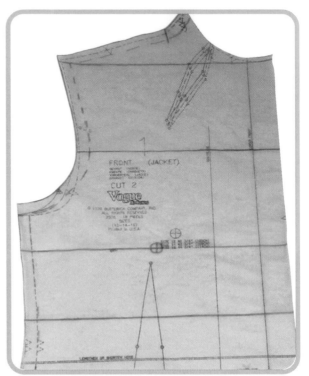

The correct cutting line for the front width at the sleeve seamline for Patty's measurements.

The photo of Patty's pattern example shows what the pattern looks like after measuring and marking. As you can see, I did not follow one size line at very many places. If I had simply looked at the back of the pattern and seen that size 16 matched Patty's bust measurement and assumed that was the correct size for her, the pattern would not have fit. This revised pattern shape looks exactly like my friend!

As you look at the pattern shape, you can see the changes I made to accommodate Patty's measurements. Most were changes to the side seams, but there were a few more detailed changes. Measurement #4 (across the upper chest, 5" down from the base of the neck) fell between the size 12 and 14 cutting line, so that's where I drew the cutting line, thus reducing the front width across this measuring line. (If you make this change, keep the sleeve from being too tight across that area by adding to the front of the sleeve approximately the same amount you reduced the jacket front, at approximately the same distance from the shoulder.)

Since the pattern across Patty's upper arm (#20) was still not wide enough, I added to the front and back of the sleeve to widen it on the full upper arm measuring line.

Widen the sleeve at the upper arm area.

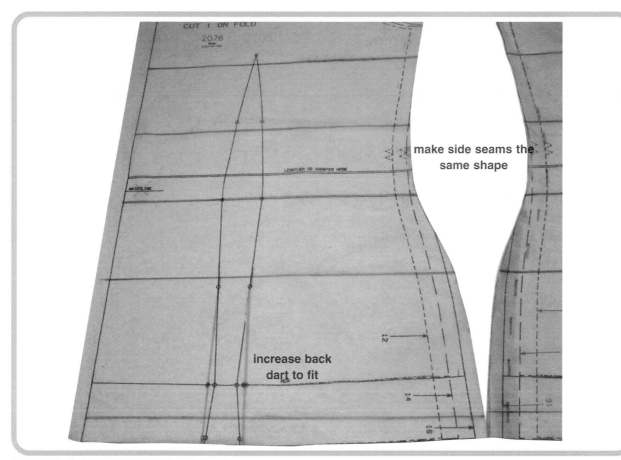

CUT 1 ON FOLD
2076

make side seams the same shape

increase back dart to fit

The back dart was increased so the side seams would match.

The armpit depth on the pattern (#30a and #30b) was deeper than Patty's measurement so I raised the armhole ⅝". I raised the back piece and the sleeve piece the same amount (see page 20).

Look at the overall shape of the sleeve. As you can see, the elbow, forearm, and hem width were too narrow, so I added the necessary amount. I measured an existing jacket sleeve width that Patty liked.

Because the side seam shapes match, the pattern measurement was a bit large in the hips but the fullness was needed at the side seams. I left the side seams as is and increased the depth of the back darts because Patty is flat across the hips.

Once you get used to doing patterns this way, you won't be able to imagine doing anything else. In all my years of couture sewing, I never made muslins, even when cutting into very expensive fabric. I measured my client, measured the pattern with this system, and always used the larger, longer number with great success. I got to the point where I could make garments for my clients with no fittings after I had made the pattern for them a couple of times. You will be able to do this too!

5

SLEEVE (JACKET)

CUT 2
2076

The final shape of the sleeve pattern.

 ake a Pattern from Your Favorite Pair of Pants
(Without Taking Them Apart!)

Do you own a pair of pants that fits so well you would love to duplicate the pattern and make more just like them? Or perhaps you have a pair that isn't quite a perfect fit, but would be with just a few changes. It's likely that these pants are too expensive to take apart and that you don't want to sacrifice them to make a pattern. With my method, you won't have to!

With pants, the area of fit most crucial is from the waist to the knee, excluding the waistband fit. The length, pant leg shape, and width don't matter. If the pants aren't a perfect fit in these areas, you can pin them to fit and apply the changes when making your pattern.

Anna's Tip About Jeans

If you want your final pattern to be dress pants, don't copy jeans or jean-style pants. I don't recommend using jean-style pants for a master pattern. Every pattern I've seen made from jeans turned out to be too small and carried all the properties of jeans – the twist in the leg, the smile below the hips, and the waistline fit. If you want a pair of pants that fits like jeans, take particular notice of the fit of the jeans you are copying. When reproducing a jean-style pant, try to match the weight of the fabric to the jeans you are copying. Measure the jeans after you have worn them and they are comfortable. If you measure the jeans after washing, but before wearing, the pattern will be too small.

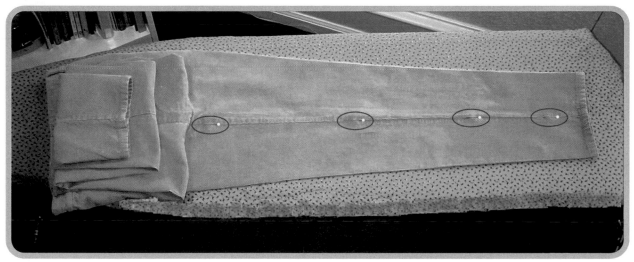

Pin and press your pants for marking.

It's best to work with a pair of pants with a flat front, but you can use a pair with a pleated front. If you choose to copy a pair made with a stretch fiber, the new pair should be made from the same type of fabric, with a similar amount of stretch. If you use your pattern to make pants from nonstretch fabric, the pants may be a bit small. This is one of the reasons for generous seam allowances.

Your goal is to get the basic shape of the pant pattern, then fine tune it. If necessary, you will pin fit the pair of pants to be copied. You will create a grid on your pants and draw a matching grid on a piece of pattern paper. You will take measurements at specific places on the pants and transfer these measurements to the pattern paper in the same places. You will add generous seam allowances to the pattern, then cut the trial pants out of muslin and baste the seams. After fitting and marking, you will take apart the trial pants and make the first pattern. (Don't be dismayed at the term "first" – every great garment, even in the largest fashion houses, starts with a first pattern.)

Step 1 – Check the Fit of the Pants You Are Copying

If necessary, try on and pin-fit the pants you have chosen to copy. Either leave the pins in and then measure the pants, or record the changes, take the pins out, and then measure your pants. If you choose the latter, you will make changes to the pattern after copying the pants. Pay close attention to the tummy, crotch (or rise), hip, and thigh areas. A change to the waistband fit is

easy to do later. In the pant construction chapter (page 73), you will learn how to finish the waistband like men's trousers that are easily adjusted through the center back.

See Troubleshooting the Fit (page 44) for help with fitting the pants you are copying. This section will also be helpful when fitting your muslin trial pair. As I mentioned before, it's best to copy a pair of pants with a flat front, but if you are copying pleated pants, slip them on and pin the pleats closed. When measuring the pants, treat the pant front as if the pleats weren't there. You can add the pleats after you've made your master pattern.

Step 2 – Press Your Pants for Marking

On the ironing board, fold each pant leg so the inseam and side seam are aligned. With the pant front facing you, fold the top leg out of the way and pin the inseam and the side seams together, through all thicknesses. Press the crease lines, front and back, stopping at the hip area.

Anna's Tip

Matching the inseam and the side seam ensures that the grain line will fall in the correct place for pressing.

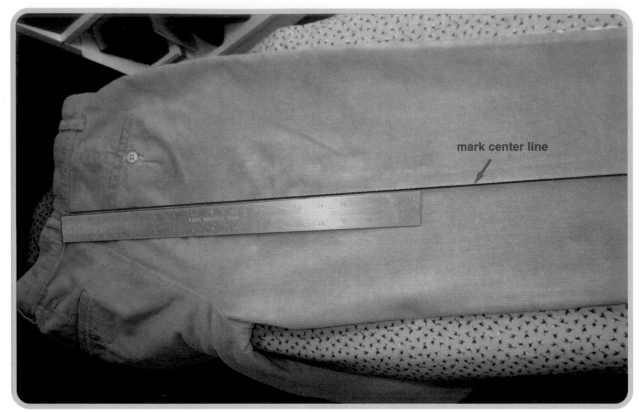

mark center line

Mark the center line to the waistline.

Step 3 – Mark the Center Front and Back

Use pins, a water-soluble marker, or chalk to mark the crease line you just pressed on the pant *front and back*. Mark up to the point where you stopped pressing the crease line.

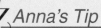
Anna's Tip

If the crease lines have been set by a dry cleaner and are not centered, pin or mark the correct lines. You may not want to reset them.

Lay an 18" or 36" ruler on the newly marked line, placing one end of the ruler just below the waistband (or where the waistline seam is located). Line up the edge of the ruler on the center line of the pant front and back. Draw a line along the edge of the ruler to extend the center line to the waistline.

This extended line may end on the center seam or anywhere between the back center seam or the side seam. Don't worry about where the line ends. This entire line will be the main line of reference on the front and the back. Label it "center line."

Anna's Tip

If you have pinned the pleats closed, pretend they aren't there and proceed.

Step 4 – Mark Horizontal Grid Lines on Your Pants

Use a water-soluble marker or chalk to mark lines at the following places on the pant *front and back*.

1 Place the pants flat on a table so the crotch seam/inseam intersection is visible. Draw a straight crotch line across the pant, starting at the crotch seam/inseam intersection and extending to the side seam. Make the line perpendicular to the center line.

2 Measuring up from the crotch line, draw parallel lines at the following places:

- 3" up from the crotch line
- 6" up from the crotch line
- 9" up from the crotch line (if needed)

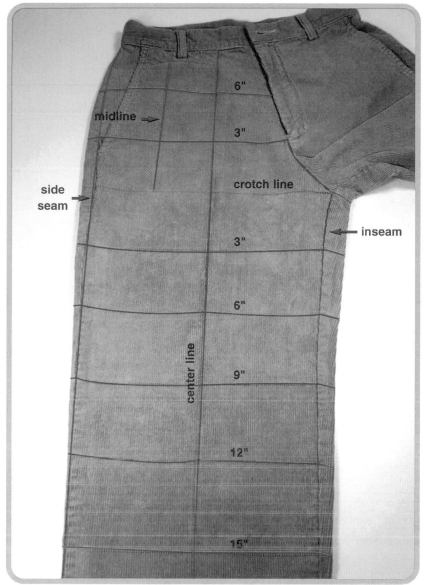

The pant front with the appropriate lines drawn.

3 Measuring down from the crotch line, draw parallel lines at the following places:

- 3" down from the crotch line
- 6" down from the crotch line
- 9" down from the crotch line
- 12" down from the crotch line
- 15" down from the crotch line

4 Draw a vertical line midway between the center line and the side seam. Begin drawing at the crotch line and extend upward to the waistline seam. You will use this line to define the placement of the waistline seam.

5 Repeat these line markings on the pants back. When you are working on the back, the side seam will be turned under.

Anna's Tip

You may want to add more measuring lines to your pants and to the grid on the pattern paper to achieve a more accurate shape.

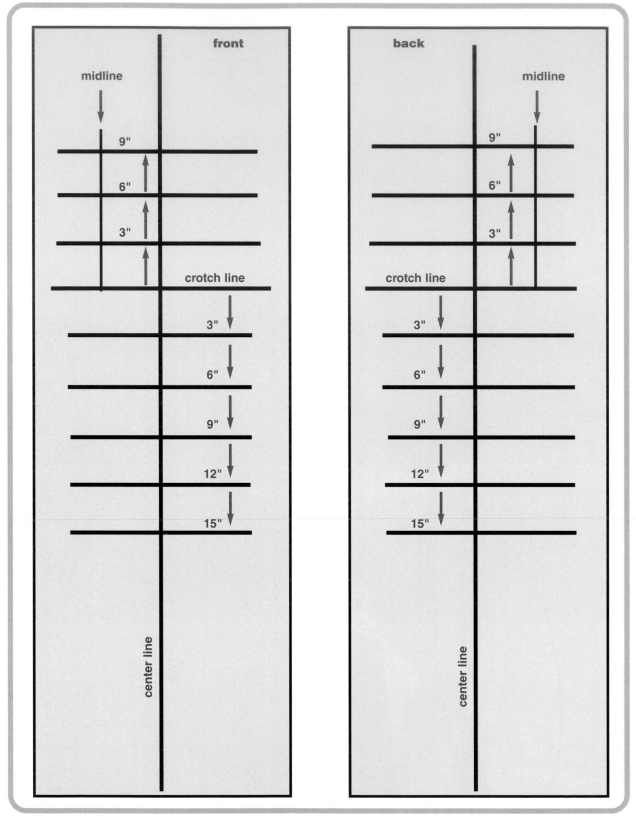

Pattern paper with the measuring lines drawn to match the lines on the pants.

Step 5 – Mark the Pattern Paper

You'll need two pieces of pattern paper long and wide enough to draw one pant pattern piece on each.

1 Draw a vertical line down the center of each piece of pattern paper.

2 On each piece of paper, draw a horizontal line approximately where the crotch line will be, about 15" down from the top of the paper.

3 Draw two parallel lines, one 3" and one 6" up from crotch, the same as you did on the pants. If you have a high waist, you may want to add another line 8" or 9" above the crotch line.

4 Draw parallel lines 3", 6", 9", 12", and 15" down from the crotch line.

5 Draw a vertical line midway between the center line and the side seam, as shown on the illustration.

6 Write "front" on the paper with the midline to the left of the center line. Write "back" on the piece with the midline to the right of the center line.

Step 6 – Measure the Pants and Draw the Pattern

This exercise will help you get the basic shape and approximate fit of your pants. For the sample, I used a pair of Eddie Bauer pants I wanted to copy. I have trouble being fit in the waist and legs – if the waist fits, the hips and legs are too big and if the hip/legs fit, the waist is too small. Since it is hard to change the waist on ready-made pants, I usually buy ones that fit the waist and take in the legs. The Eddie Bauer pants fit in the waist, so I took in the hips and legs.

Note: The following instructions refer to the front, which is pictured. Repeat the same steps for the back. It makes no difference which you do first.

Anna's Tip

If you are in doubt about a measurement, choose the larger, longer, or wider number. Remember, you will be working on cotton, not cashmere!

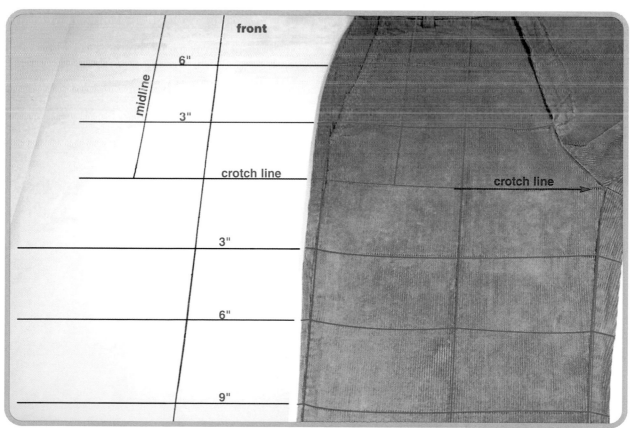

Lay the pattern paper front next to the pants front.

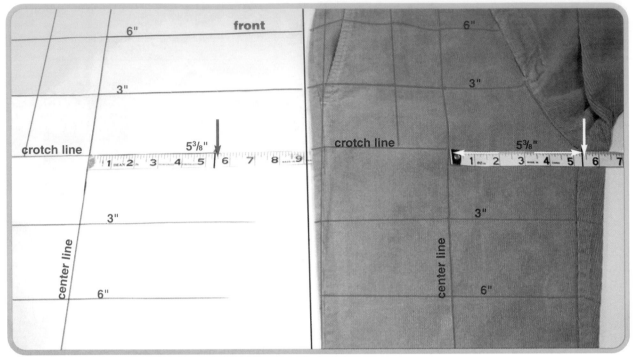

Measure and mark the distance from the center line to the crotch seamline.

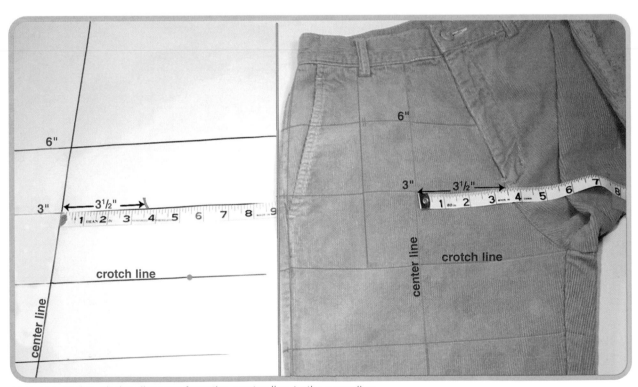

Measure and mark the distance from the center line to the seamline.

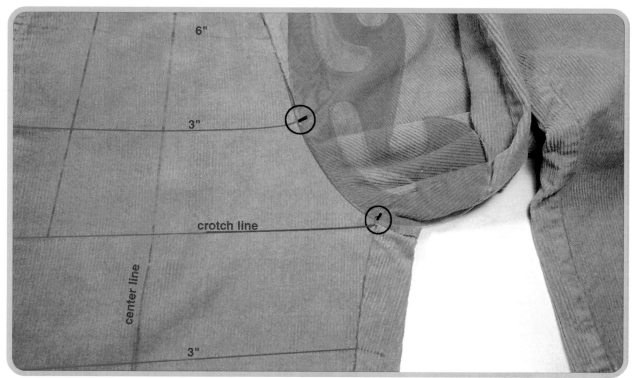

Define the shape of the crotch seam using a French curve.

Mark the Center Front Seamline

1 Lay the pant front next to the pattern paper labeled "front."

2 On the pants, place a tape measure at the point where the crotch line and center line intersect. Measure the distance from the center line to the crotch seamline (the intersection of the inseam and the crotch seam). In the sample, this measurement is 5⅜". Make a mark on the pattern paper at the corresponding spot.

Move the tape measure to the intersection of the center line and the 3" line above the crotch line. Measure the distance from the center line to the seamline. In the sample, that measurement is 3½". Make a mark on the pattern paper at the correct spot.

3 Move the tape measure to the intersection of the center line and the 6" line above the crotch line. Measure the distance from the center line to the seamline. Make a mark on the pattern paper at the correct spot. Repeat on the 9" line above the crotch line if applicable.

4 Define the shape of the crotch seam by using a French curve, a curved ruler, or tracing paper. If you use a French curve or curved ruler, find the area on the ruler that matches the curve of the crotch seamline. Make two marks on the ruler, one where the crotch seam begins at the top of the inseam, and one at the 3" line.

Place the French curve or curved ruler on the pattern paper in the corresponding position. Trace along the edge of the curve to mark the shape of the seamline on the pattern paper. You may also use a piece of tracing paper to copy the curve of the seam.

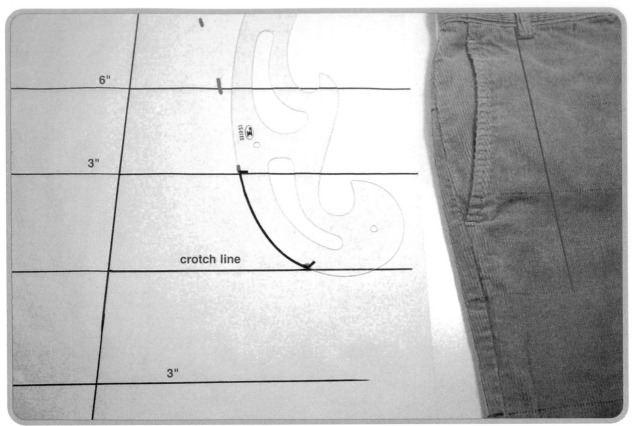

Transfer the crotch seam shape to the pattern paper.

Measure and mark the center front seam length.

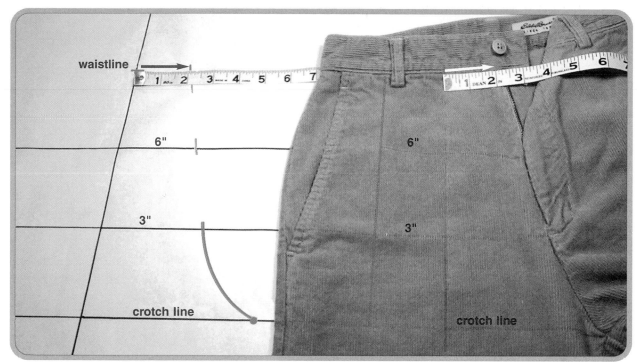

Mark the center front seamline at the waistline.

5 To find the length of the center front seam, use a tape measure or curved ruler to measure from the crotch seam where it intersects the inseam to the top of the pants where the waistline seam is located. Follow the curve of the seam to get the maximum length. Mark the pattern paper along the curve.

6 Measure from the center line to the center of the front zipper on the waistline seam, just below the waistband. Make a mark on the pattern paper in the correct spot.

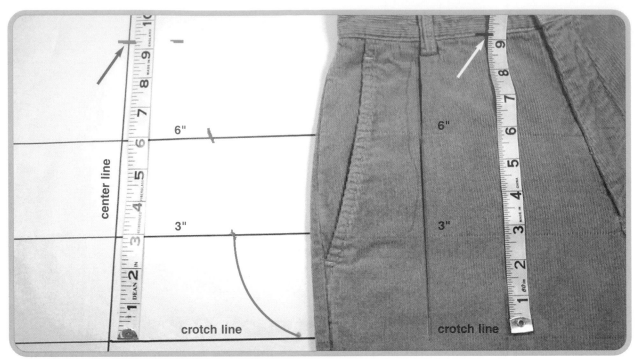

Measure and mark the waistline seam height on the center line.

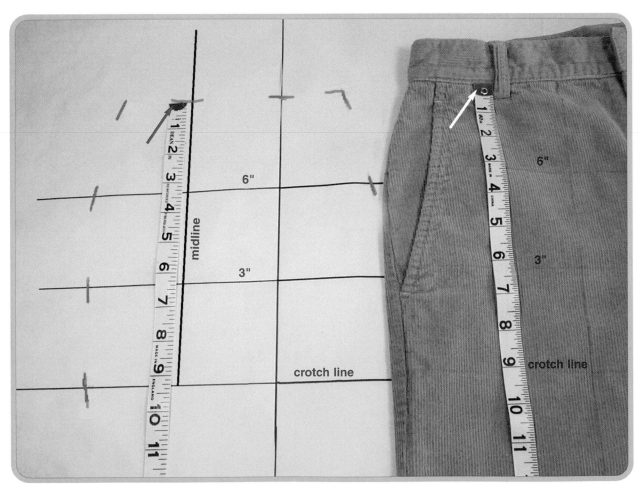

Measure and mark the waistline seam height on the midline.

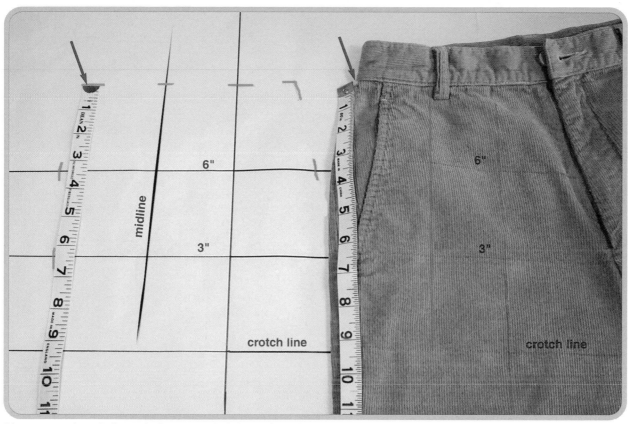

Measure and mark the waistline seam height on the side seam.

Mark the Waistline Seam

1 On the pants, measure the distance from the crotch line to the waistline seam on the center line. Mark the waistline seam placement on the pattern paper.

2 On the pants, measure the distance from the crotch line to the waistline seam on the midline. Mark the waistline seam placement on the pattern paper.

3 On the pants, measure the distance from the crotch line to the waistline seam at the side seam. Mark the waistline seam on the pattern paper.

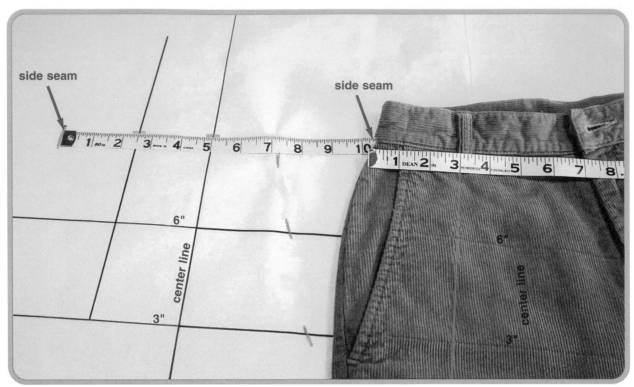

Mark the waistline side seam placement.

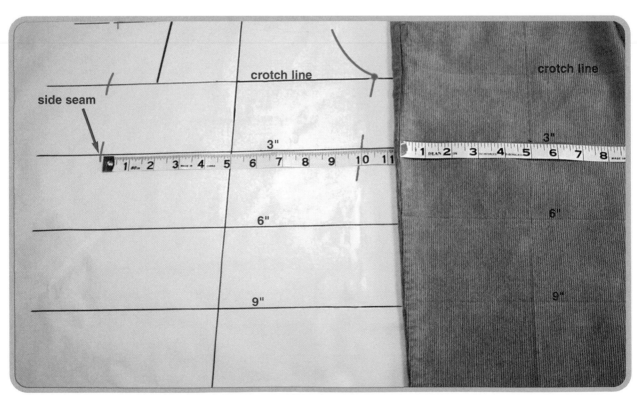

Measure and mark the side seam down the length of the leg.

Mark the Waistline Width from the Center Seam to the Side Seam

1 On the pants, measure the distance from the center line to the side seam at the waistline. Mark the seamline on the pattern paper.

2 Mark the side seam above the crotch line on the 9" line (if applicable), the 6" line, the 3" line, and the crotch line.

3 Mark the side seam on all the horizontal lines below the crotch line. The center line should be half the total distance across the pant leg.

Mark the Hemline

1 Measure the length of the inseam and mark it on the pattern paper.

2 Measure the length of the side seam and mark it on the pattern paper.

Connect the Dots

1 After making all your marks, sketch lines to connect the marks. Don't worry if your lines aren't perfect. You will straighten them later.

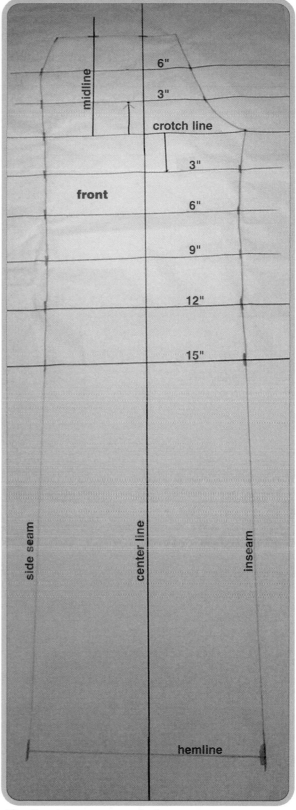

After the dots are connected.

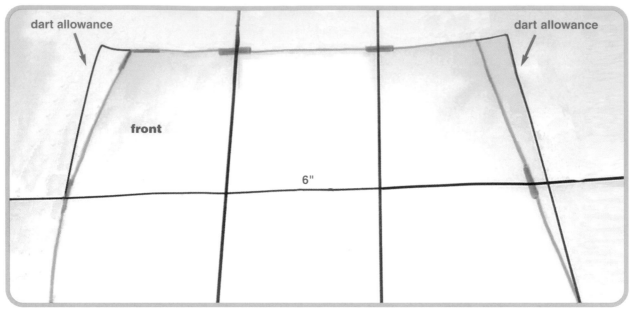

Add allowances for darts at the side seam and center seam.

Step 7 – Allow for the Darts

1 Measure the length and width of the darts on the pants you are copying. Add half the total amounts of the darts to the side seam and half to the center seam.

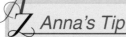 *Anna's Tip*

If you want darts and are working with pleated pants (with the pleats pinned closed), add approximately 1" to the side seam and 1" to the center seam. You will pin the darts in at the proper places and fit the waist during your fitting. If you are working with pleated pants and only want to make pleated pants, don't add to the side seam or center seam. You will add the pleats after your pattern is made.

2 After adding for the darts, if the center front seam above the curve is not on the straight of grain, draw the pattern so that it is on the straight of the grain. Adding the allowance for darts will help straighten the seamline if it is not on the grain. Don't worry if you change the waistline measurement – you will fit the waist later.

Step 8 – Troubleshoot Funny Marks

If your pattern looks oddly shaped, don't panic. Garments can lose their original shape with wear, even after washing or dry cleaning. Remember that you are making a trial pair. This is just the first step.

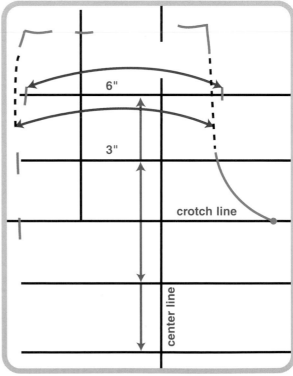

These two marks are out of line. Move them both so they line up with the other seamline marks.

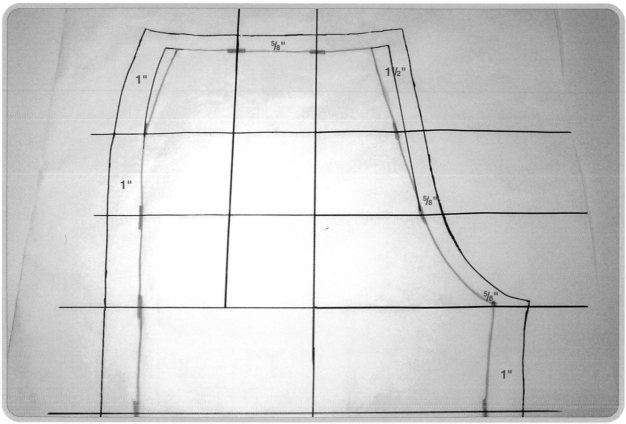

Add allowances for darts at the side seam and center seam.

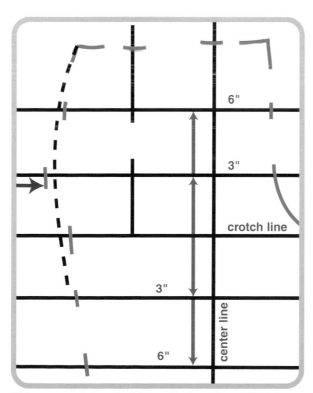

This one mark is out of line with the others. Sketch a seam line that averages the difference.

1 If you have more than one mark that looks odd, chances are there is another mark out of line across the pattern on the same measuring line. Simply move both marks so they are brought back in line with the other marks.

2 If you have one stray mark along the seamline, re-mark it so it's in line with the marks above and below it. If you only have one mark that looks suspicious, measure again. If it's correct, check the marks above and below. If they are right, sketch a line that averages two or three seamline marks.

Step 9 – Add Seam Allowances

1 Add seam allowances around the entire pattern as follows:

- add ⅝" to the waist seam
- add ⅝" to the center front seam
- add ⅝" to the center back seam to about ⅓ the way up, then deepen the seam to 1½"
- add 1" to the side seams
- add 1" to the inseams

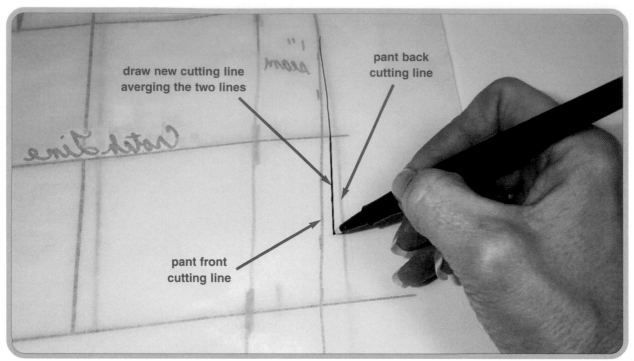

draw new cutting line
averging the two lines

pant back
cutting line

pant front
cutting line

The two purple lines are out of line. Average them both so they line up with the other seamline marks.

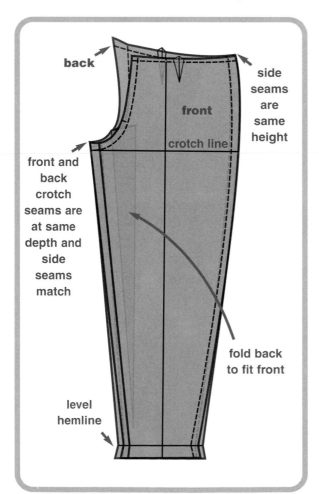

back

side
seams
are
same
height

front

crotch line

front and
back
crotch
seams are
at same
depth and
side
seams
match

fold back
to fit front

level
hemline

Make the waistline seams and crotch seams the same height.

Step 10 – Match the Front and Back Pieces

This is my favorite part!

1 Lay the front pattern piece on top of the back. Match the side seams first. If the front seam and back seam are not the same shape, simply sketch a new line, averaging the two.

You want the seamlines to be the same shape, so cut the front and back side seams together. The inseams may differ slightly in shape, which is fine, so cut them separately.

2 Vertically fold the back piece between the center line and the inseam so it is approximately the same size as the front piece.

3 Check to see that the crotch seam and the side seams line up, heightwise. If there's a large discrepancy between the seam heights, average the two (raise one by half and lower the other the same amount). Sketch a line that will blend the new height with the original seamline. You may want to raise the lower seam, especially on the waistline.

Anna's Tip

If the two crotch seams are not level, you will be guaranteed a twist in the leg.

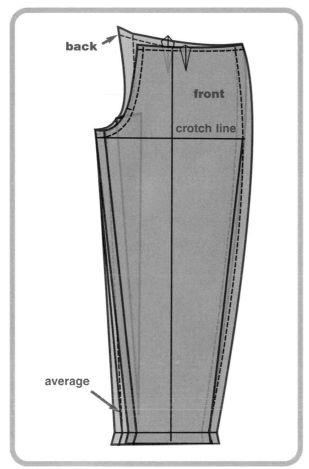

The red lines are an average of the two seamlines.

4 Check the lower pant leg to make sure the pant legs don't veer off in different directions. I doubt this will happen, but I have had the problem on a pattern taken from jeans. If the pant front and back lower legs don't match, sketch new lines to make them match, averaging the two seamlines.

5 Straighten the seamlines by using a French curve, a curved ruler, or by sketching the lines.

6 While your pattern pieces are matched, add notches along the side seams and on the inseams (or anywhere else you desire).

7 With the front and back pieces still together, fold them in half lengthwise and square the hem. Don't worry if they are too short or too long at this time.

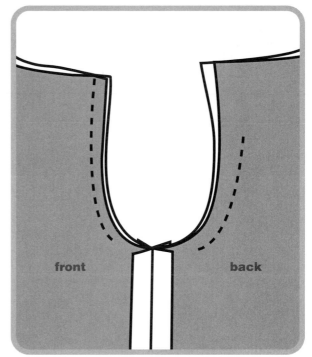

Baste the center front and back seams, then the inseams.

Step 11 – Cut, Mark, and Baste Your Trial Pants

1 Using the new pattern, cut the trial pants from muslin, using the center lines on the front and back as the grain lines.

2 Write "front" and "back" on the appropriate cut fabric pieces. Mark the center back seamline since it is not a consistent width. (I once had a student who forgot to mark her front and back pieces and did her fitting wearing them backwards. We all had a good laugh, then fixed them!)

3 Baste the center front seam, stopping 2½" before reaching the inseam.

4 Baste the center back seam, starting 2½" from the inseam and stopping approximately 7" from the top of the waistline.

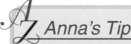 *Anna's Tip*

Remember that the center front seam is ⅝", as is the center back seam in the curved area.

Note: *Muslin can be confusing, so sew the center front and center back first to ensure that you won't connect the wrong pieces. (You don't want to make a skirt!) Don't sew the entire length of the center seams because you want to be able to sew the inseams, then sew your crotch seam.*

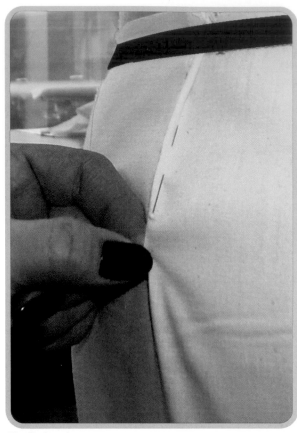

5 Baste the inseams and the side seams, remembering that they are 1" seams. Press the seams open.

6 Baste across the area of the crotch seam that was left open.

7 Press the muslin as if it were your best pair of pants, even setting a crease line.

Step 12 – Fit the Trial Pair

This is a really good time to grab a sewing friend to help with the fitting.

1 Put on the trial pants and pull the rise/crotch into place. Pin the center back seam closed to the waistline.

2 Pin-fit the darts. You may find that two darts to a side work better than one. Adjust the side seams at the waistline. You may need to adjust the side seams and darts to get the best fit.

3 Secure the waistline with a string, a piece of elastic, a narrow belt, or a tape measure. (If you use elastic, don't pull it too tight.)

4 Mark the waistline below the string, elastic, or belt. This is your waistline seam.

Pin-fit the darts.

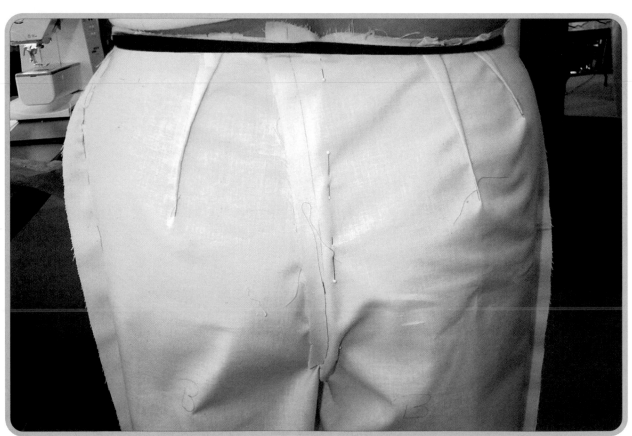

On this trial pair, one dart works better than two.

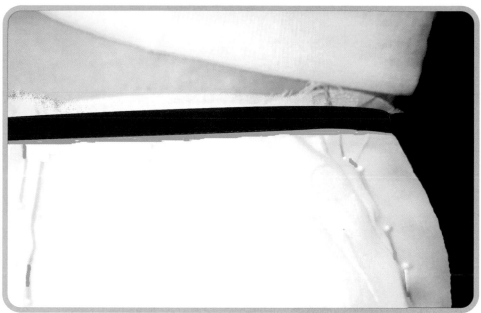

Mark the waistline seam below the elastic.

5 Pin the approximate hemline.

6 Mark a large "X" on one front fabric piece and one back fabric piece. You will use these pieces to make your first pattern.

Anna's Tip

If your body is asymmetrical, choose the side that is larger, longer, or higher to use as the master pattern and re-cut the other front and back pieces to accommodate your individual differences. You may prefer to have four separate pattern pieces.

Step 13 – Check the Fit

1 Check to see that the side seams are in the center of your body. If not, mark the proper place and make changes to the pattern. If you need to shift them, simply take off what is necessary from one seam and add it to the adjoining seam, thus shifting its placement.

2 Make sure the rise/crotch is close to your body, but not touching. It should be about 1" lower than your body, or wherever is comfortable for you. Remember that the rise/crotch seam is on the bias and will stretch and move away from your body with wear. Keep this in mind when fitting. I like to have a close fit at first and let the rise/crotch drop with wear. If the pants will be dry cleaned, the rise/crotch should remain as it was after your first wearing. If you will wash the pants, the rise/crotch will tighten up and then drop again while wearing, like jeans. (This is detailed on page 45.)

3 Sit down to check the waistline seam placement, how the rise/crotch fits, and the waist circumference.

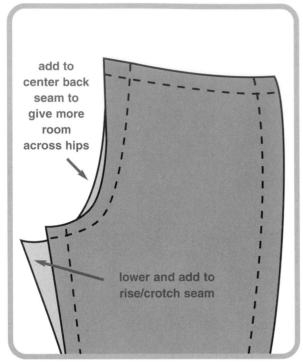

add to center back seam to give more room across hips

lower and add to rise/crotch seam

The piece on top is the general shape of a pant back pattern that causes smiles.

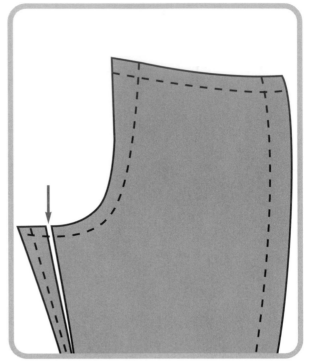

The alteration for fullness in the pant back, just below the hip line.

Step 14 – Solve Fit Problems

Problem: Smile lines below the buttocks (like on most jeans).

Solution: Smile lines occur when the back rise/crotch seam is too short and the pant is not wide enough across the hips at the top of the inseam. To remedy this, add to the back inseam at the rise/crotch, which also lengthens the rise/crotch seam. You may also want to add to the center back seam for additional room across the hip line. I prefer to draw the alterations, but the slash and pivot method will give you the same results. Knowing how much to add is the trick! If you are able to open the center back seam and the inseam from the knee to the top of the inseam, you will be able to measure how much you need to add. Don't forget to lower the front rise/crotch seam the same amount as you did on the back seam.

Problem: Fullness in the pant leg (vertically) in the back, just below the hips.

Solution: This calls for an alteration that will take the fullness out of the pant through the back inseam only. I usually pinch a vertical tuck in the area of fullness on the back leg to the inside of the center crease line. Then I take that amount off the inseam at the rise/crotch. (This alteration is the opposite of taking the smile out of the pant back.)

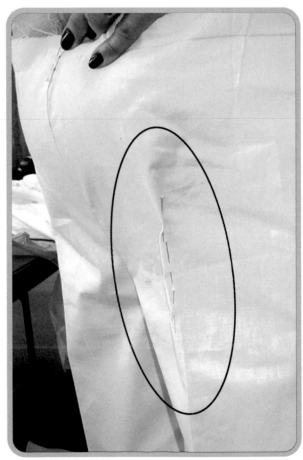

Reduce excess in the groin area by pinning a dart in the pant.

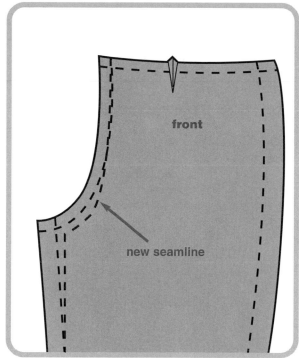

The new seamline shape reduces fullness at the groin.

Problem: Indent at your groin (or too much fullness in the pant below the tummy at the groin area).

Solution: There are two ways to fix this:

1 Pinch and pin a vertical dart beginning at the place that has too much fullness. Pin the dart until it reduces to nothing. Press the dart flat and pretend it isn't there.

2 You can either redraw the pattern, taking out the amount you pinned, or press the dart until it reduces to nothing, baste it flat, and pretend it doesn't exist. Both methods correct the shape of the pattern.

Problem: Vertical lines or folds in the pant legs, front and back.

Solution: This occurs when there is too much fullness in the pant leg. Take in equally on the inseams and the side seams. This will keep the centers on line.

Problem: Rise/crotch seam is too low.

Solution: Pull the pants up to the proper place, re-mark and reset the waistband. Refit the side seams. Transfer the alterations to the pattern by repeating the alterations you did to the pants, or redraw the pattern and only raise the rise/crotch seam. It's good to do this when the waist and hip area are a good fit.

Problem: Rise/crotch seam is too high or too close to the body.

Solution: Wearing the trial pair, mark the spot on the front and/or back where the rise/crotch begins to touch your body. Take them off and redraw the rise/crotch curve, moving it away from your body. Start with a ¼" alteration and fit again. Continue this process until they are comfortable.

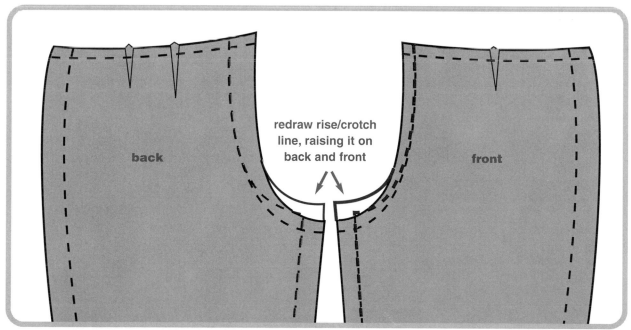

Raise the rise/crotch on the pattern.

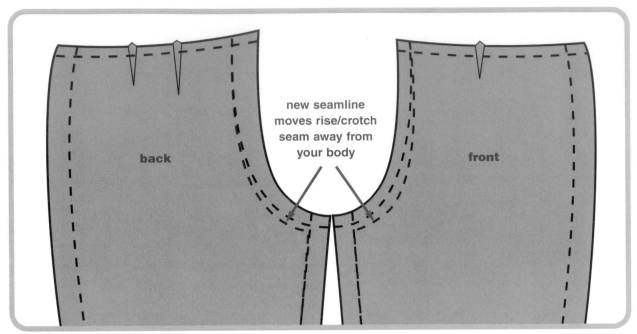

Lower the rise/crotch seam on the pattern.

**Anna's Tip**

Remember, the rise/crotch seam is on the bias and will stretch and move away from your body with wear within a day's time.

Problem: Too much fullness across the hip at the center back seam.

Solution: Take in the center back seam until it begins to take the shape of your body.

Step 15 – Make Your First Pattern from the Trial Pair

1 Take apart the trial pants and use only one front and one back piece.

2 Draw around the outer edges of the pieces on new pattern paper.

3 Mark the grain line (center line), the darts, the seamlines, the center back seamline, the notches, and any other markings you want.

4 Make any changes you discovered during your fitting.

5 Leave the 1" side seams and inseams.

Adjust the center back seam for a perfect fit.

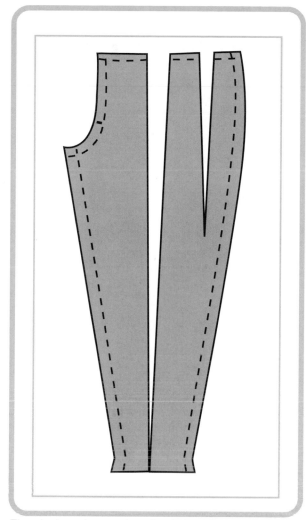

The slash and spread method of adding pleats.

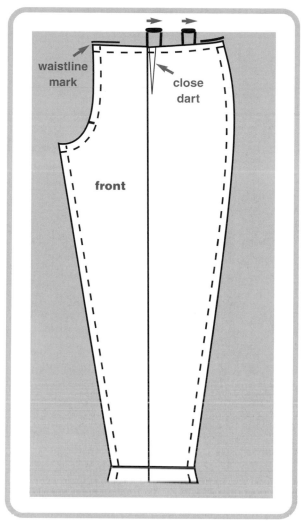

Pleat the paper first.

Step 16 – Change the Style

Pleated Pants – Two Methods

Method 1: Copy, Slash, and Spread

1 Close the front dart or darts and trace the pattern on new pattern paper. Be sure to mark the center front line.

2 After determining the size of the pleats you prefer, slash the pattern on the center line all the way to the hemline. Spread the pattern. There will usually be 2½" to 4" total allowed for the pleats. The pleat nearest the center is the deeper pleat, usually 1½" to 2", and the second pleat is usually ¼" to ½" smaller. Check a pair you like.

3 Repeat the process for the second pleat by making a slash approximately 1½" to 1¾" from the first pleat. Again, check a pair you like.

4 Tape the slashed pattern piece to a new piece of pattern paper.

Method 2: Pleat the Pattern Paper First

1 If you have darts on the pattern, close them. Place the flat front pattern piece on a new piece of pattern paper and trace along the top edge of the pant. Mark the center line on the new pattern paper and line it up with the original pattern.

2 Remove the original pattern. Decide on the size, direction, and placement of the pleats.

3 For pleats facing the center front, fold the pattern paper using the center line as the starting line to form the first pleat. Fold the second pleat in the pattern paper. For pleats facing the side seam, place the center line in the middle of the pleat and fold the pattern paper. Decide on the second pleat and fold the pattern paper.

4 Leaving the pleats closed on the pattern paper, lay your flat front pattern piece on the pleated paper with the center lines aligned (leave the darts closed). Since the paper will buckle a bit, trace around the flat front pattern down to where the pleated paper starts to buckle (about halfway). Open the pleats on the paper

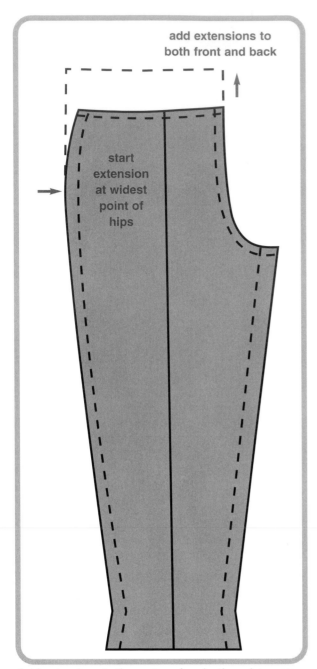

add extensions to
both front and back

start
extension
at widest
point of
hips

Add extensions to the pattern for elastic waist pants.

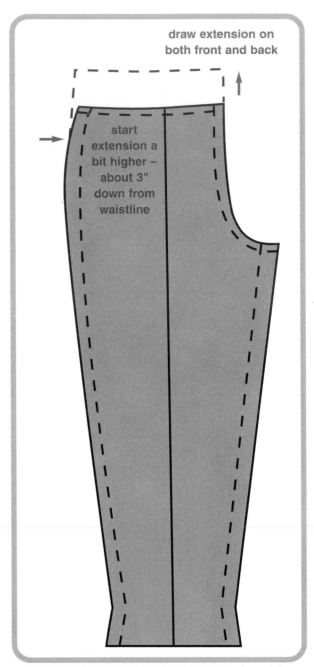

draw extension on
both front and back

start
extension a
bit higher –
about 3"
down from
waistline

Reduce the fullness of elastic waist pants by adding a zipper.

and trace around the lower half of the pant leg.

5 Mark the pleats, which are just very long darts. Leave the pleats closed when you cut the top edge. This will give you the perfect shape for cutting the pleats.

Anna's Tip

You may need to adjust these pleats to get them exactly where you want them.

Pull-On or Elastic Waist Pants

1 Cut the pattern straight up from the fullest part of the hip on the pattern front and back. From the waistline seam, add twice the width of the elastic plus ½" (the raw edge will be turned under ⅜", ⅛" is for the turn of the cloth over the elastic).

2 Since you want very little fullness at your waist, cut down the fullness by adding a side or front zipper. Even though the zipper adds work to the pant construction, it provides the comfort of an elastic waist without all the fullness.

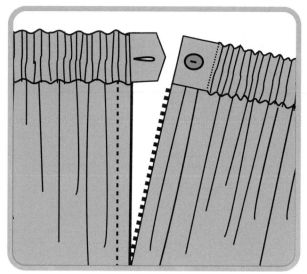

Elastic waist pants with a zipper closure.

3 Add a tab to the casing on the back side at the top of the zipper for a button. Make a buttonhole on the waistband through the elastic (or use hooks and eyes).

Slash Pocket Pants

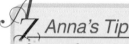 *Anna's Tip*

I use only one pattern piece for the pocket and the facing. I fold the pant pattern under on the diagonal line, forming the pocket edge.

1 Close the darts or pleats.

2 On the pant front, draw a line from the waistline about 1" to 1½" in from the side seam and angle it down the pant about 6" to 7" deep, ending on the side seam cutting line of the pant. (Measure some existing pants with this type of pocket to see where you want the slash pocket.) This line is where you want the pocket to end.

3 Add a ¼" seam allowance to the *outside edge* (toward the side seam) of the pocket line you just drew.

4 The new line you drew, with an added ¼" seam allowance, becomes the cutting/fold line on the pocket facing and on the pant front for slash pocket style pants.

5 Use a piece of pattern paper large enough to make the pocket pattern. Trace along the side and across the top edge of the pant front to get the shape of the pants. Be sure the pleats or darts are still closed.

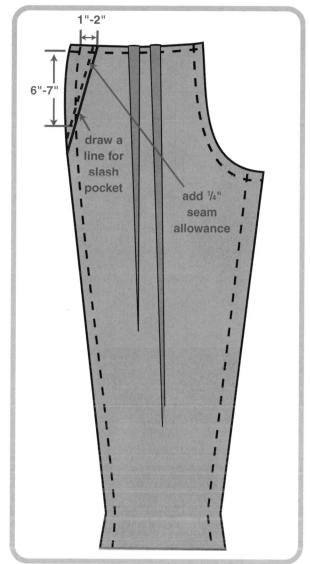

1"-2"

6"-7"

draw a line for slash pocket

add ¼" seam allowance

The slash pocket line and seam allowance are shown in red.

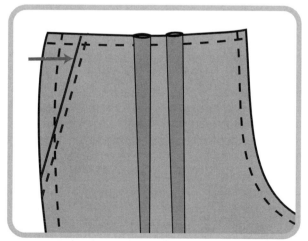

The new cutting/fold line is shown in red.

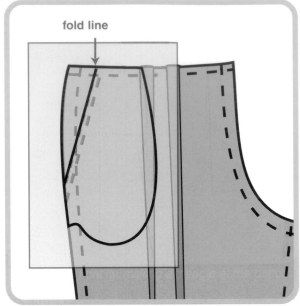

fold line

Trace around the pant top edge and side on new pattern paper to make a pocket pattern. Draw or copy a pocket shape. Draw in the fold line on the pocket pattern.

6 Draw the remainder of the pocket (or copy one from an existing pattern), using your own pant pattern side and top edge lines.

7 Draw the fold line from the pant front on the pocket pattern.

8 For the pocket facing, turn the pocket pattern under on the fold line and cut two.

9 Cut two each for the pocket pieces.

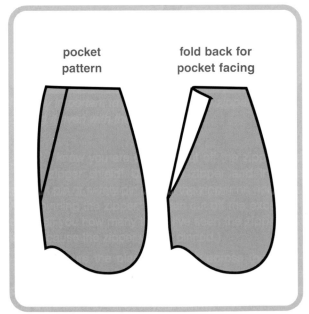

pocket pattern   fold back for pocket facing

Use one pattern piece for the pocket and the facing.

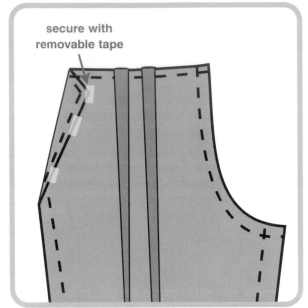

secure with removable tape

Fold back the pattern on the fold line for slash pocket style pants.

10 When cutting the pant front for a slash pocket, turn the pattern back on the fold line and secure it with removable tape. For styles without a slash pocket, leave it unfolded.

Step 17 – Things to Remember When Making Your First Pair of Pants from Your New Pattern

1 Leave a 1" seam allowance on the side seams and inseams in case you need additional ease in different fabrics. When you are confident about the fit and pattern, you can make your seams ⅝" or leave them at 1" for insurance.

2 For your first pair of pants, use a medium-weight fabric without much drape, such as cotton twill or lightweight denim. As you make additional pairs, you will perfect the pattern until you can cut, sew, and go!

3 The exercise you just did is the first step to getting a perfect pair of pants. If your first pair is not perfect, make the necessary alterations and transfer the changes to your pattern. Make another trial pair from the pattern with the changes. When I design and make pants for my clients, I usually make the pants and tweak the pattern three times. I can guarantee the pants you make from your new pattern will be better than those made from any commercial pattern (unless you were the model for whom the pattern was made).

Chapter 3

Master the Art of Pant Construction

Now that you have a custom-fit pant pattern, it's time to sew your first pair of pants. Wear the first pair a few times and see if there are changes you want to make to the pattern. After you have perfected the pattern you will be able to make a pair of pants in the same time it takes to go shopping and try on a dozen pair that don't fit.

For the first pair, I recommend using inexpensive, medium-weight fabric that is easy to work with.

Step 1 – Prepare the Fabric and Cut Out the Pants

1 Needless to say, preshrink your fabric! If it is 100% cotton, preshrink it up to three times. If you are using a nice wool, either have it dry cleaned or steam it carefully before cutting. Preshrink all other fabrics in the same way you will treat them after you have made the pants.

2 Lay out your pant front and back pieces on the fabric. Allow for the waistband pieces, pocket pieces, and belt loop pieces. For the pocket pattern pieces, refer to page 50. If you are putting in angled welt pockets on the pants front, refer to pages 56 to 58 in this chapter.

3 Make a pattern piece for the waistband to be cut on double thickness. The width of this piece should be twice the *finished* desired waistband width plus $7/8$". The length should be 4" to 5" longer than half of your waistline measurement. This is a split waistband and will be finished at the center back. Cut these pieces lengthwise or crosswise. This is longer than you need, but by doing it this way you don't have to think about it!

4 Make a pattern piece long enough for the belt loops. Don't forget to add the necessary seam allowances to be sewn into the waistband and the amount needed to turn under at the top of the waistband. Determine the finished belt loop width and double it, then add $1/2$" (for $1/4$" seams). To determine the length of the belt loop, measure the width of a belt you like and allow for the turn of the cloth over the belt's thickness.

For example, to make seven belt loops for a finished $1^1/4$" wide waistband (two front, two side, two back, and one center back), the pattern piece will measure 14" long x $1^1/4$" wide. The 14" length allows 2" for each of the seven belt loops. If you cut the strip $1^1/4$" wide, you can fold it in half lengthwise and stitch it using a $1/4$" seam allowance. This will give you $3/8$" wide belt loops. Now you have a formula for the belt loops to be used every time you need to make them.

5 Pin all the pattern pieces to the fabric and cut out the pants, pocket pieces, belt loops, and waistband pieces.

6 Mark the pant front dart or pleats, back darts, and center back seamline.

7 Set aside the curved fabric pieces that are left after cutting the front pieces. You will use them later for the facings and the zipper shield.

Step 2 – Set the Pleats

1 If your pants have pleats, now is the time to soft set them. If you want to make front vertical or angled welt pockets, soft setting the pleats now will help you decide where to place the pockets. Fold the pant fronts in half lengthwise, lining up the side seam with the inseam and press a soft crease up to the crotch.

2 Pin the pleats and make sure the center crease line is in line with or fairly close to the first pleat. (The first pleat is the pleat closest to the center front.)

3 Hold one pant front up to your body to see how the pleats fall. Adjust the placement of the pleats if necessary.

Step 3 – Make the Pockets (Slash, Welt, or Faux Welt)

Slash Pockets

Most patterns give good instructions for slash pockets. The only difference I recommend is to use ¼" seam allowances so you won't be slowed down by trimming later.

1 See page 50 for instructions for making a pocket pattern. Reinforce the pocket seamline with twill tape or fusible straight tape. This will help keep the pocket edge from stretching, as it is cut slightly on the bias and would stretch a bit more with use. The pocket edge on the pant pattern and on the pocket is set up to be a ¼" seam allowance.

2 With right sides together, place the pocket facing on the pant front and stitch the seam with a ¼" seam allowance. Understitch the pocket facing and press. Edgestitch or topstitch the pocket.

> *A Anna's Tip*
>
> **To understitch, fold or press the seam allowance toward the facing and edgestitch the seam from the right side of the pocket. This will keep the facing from rolling out. (See page 79 for details.)**

Photo by Mellisa K. Mahoney

Pleated pants can have a number of different looks. In this pair of two-pleat pants, the pleat closest to the center is inverted, like a box pleat. This detail adds interest to the pant front and the pleat lays close to the body.

3 To keep the pocket from gaping, position the lower pocket edge ¼" beyond the side seam. This will cause the pocket to curve around your body.

4 Line up the pocket piece with the edges of the facing, with the notches at the top of the pocket. Stitch around the edges.

5 Finish the pocket edges by serging or zigzagging. (You can also make French seams to finish the pocket edges.)

The World's Easiest Welt Pocket

Vertical, horizontal, or angled

The measurements in these instructions are for finished welts ¼" wide. You will learn the formula and can change the finished width of the welts to your liking. Most welt pockets measure 5" long for hip pockets, 5½" for angled front welt pockets and jacket pockets, and 6" for men's jacket pockets.

Some of the photos and illustrations in this chapter show welt pockets made on the jacket front. It doesn't matter where you put the pockets, they are done the same way. The only variable is the shape of the pocket behind the welts, which depends on the type and location of the pocket.

1 Mark the pocket placement on the right side of the garment front using a water-soluble pen or disappearing pen. Mark the places where you want the pocket to begin and end. Make parallel marks ½" apart. If you are making jacket or pant front pockets, mark both front pieces at the same time.

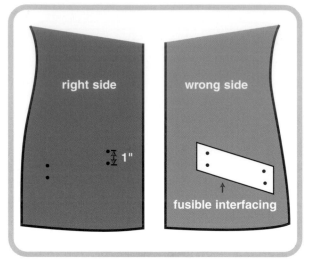

Mark the welt pocket placement and fuse interfacing to the area.

2 Press fusible tricot or a suitable fusible interfacing to the wrong side of the fabric where the pocket work will be done. The interfacing piece should extend past the parallel marks by ½" all the way around. (This is to reinforce the corners and stabilize them when you do the all-important cutting of the corners.)

3 Cut four strips of fabric (or a contrasting fabric) the length of your pocket plus 1¼" x 1" wide (four times the width of the finished welt). These strips can be cut on the bias, on the lengthwise, or on the crosswise grain. Press fusible tricot to these pieces. (You can do this before you cut them if that's easier.)

Anna's Tip

When making welts from heavy fabric, cut the welt pieces a bit wider than 1". Fold the fabric first, then cut the welt so it measures ½" wide when folded. With thicker fabric, you must allow for the turn of the cloth or the welt pieces will be too narrow and throw off the entire opening.

4 Fold the strips in half lengthwise, press, and mark the lengthwise center ⅝" from each end.

Anna's Tip

If your fabric is a dark color, use light-colored fusible interfacing so you can see your stitches from the back. It will be important to see those stitches when you cut the pocket open.

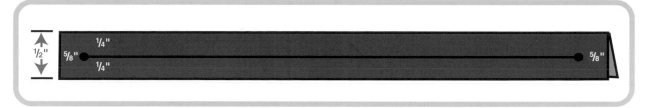

5 Place the folded, pressed welt pieces on the garment front and line up the dots. The folded edge should face the outside. The measurements are set up so the welt pieces butt together and are sewn exactly down the center of each piece. Stitch ¼" from the folded edge of the welt piece, from dot to dot, leaving ½" between the rows of stitching and backstitching on each end.

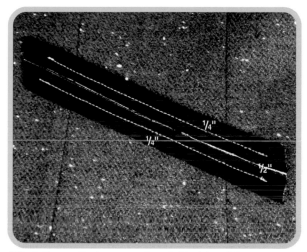

Stitch the welt pieces on the right side of the garment.

6 If you want a button loop on the back pant pocket, make the loop and pin it in the center of the pocket. After stitching the welt, stitch the button loop.

Stitch the button loop on the back pocket.

7 Check your stitching on the wrong side of the fabric. The two rows of stitching should be exactly parallel, ½" apart, and exactly the same length. If they are not the same length, decide which one is correct and adjust the other. It's important that these stitches, along with the clipping, be precise. The rest of the pocket is really easy!

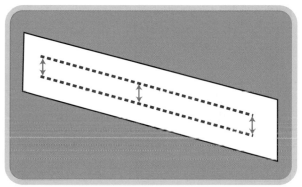

Check on the back to make sure the rows of stitching are parallel and even.

8 From the wrong side of the pant, cut the pocket open, cutting only the pant fabric layer. *Do not* cut the welts. Stop cutting ⅝" from the end of the welts.

9 Clip from the stopping point to the stitches at each end of the pocket, forming a "V". It's very important that you clip exactly to the stitches – don't cut past them and don't stop short. If you stop short, you will get a pucker and if you clip too far, you'll have to make your pocket longer to reach where you clipped. *Don't clip the stitches.*

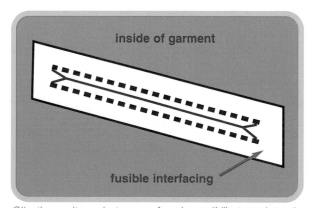

Clip the welt pocket open, forming a "V" at each end.

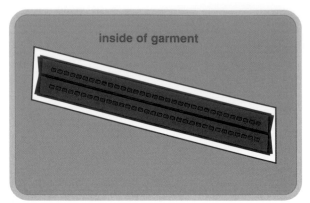

inside of garment

Pull the welt to the inside of the garment.

10 From the wrong side of the pant, pull the welt pieces to the inside. Turn the corner "V" inside and press. Grade any layers, leaving the longer layer toward the outside.

11 Stitch across the ends of the welt, backstitching for security.

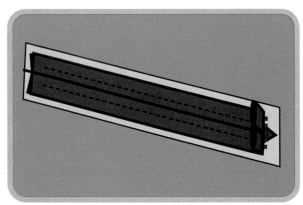

Stitch across the ends of the welt pocket.

12 Hand baste or zigzag the welts together. Leave the stitches in until the garment is finished.

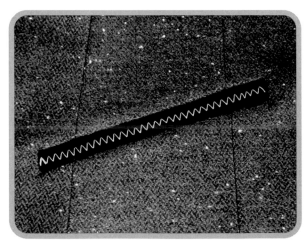

Close the welts before making the pocketing.

Make the Pocket Behind the Welts for Vertical or Angled Welt Pockets on the Pant Front

If you use fashion fabric to make the inner pocket piece, that's what will show from the outside – a very professional look.

1 Make a pocket pattern by laying a piece of pattern paper on the inside of the pant front. Draw the pocket shape, extending the pattern to the side seam and the pant waistline. (You can copy an existing pocket pattern to get the shape of the perimeter of the pocket edge, but the side seam of the pocket should match the shape of your pant side seam and waist seam.) Now is your chance to make a pocket the right size!

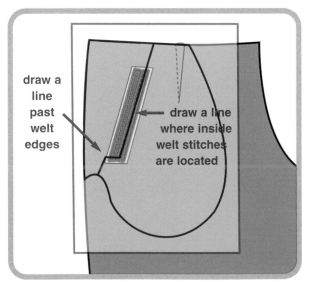

draw a line past welt edges

draw a line where inside welt stitches are located

Make a pocket pattern for the angled welt pockets.

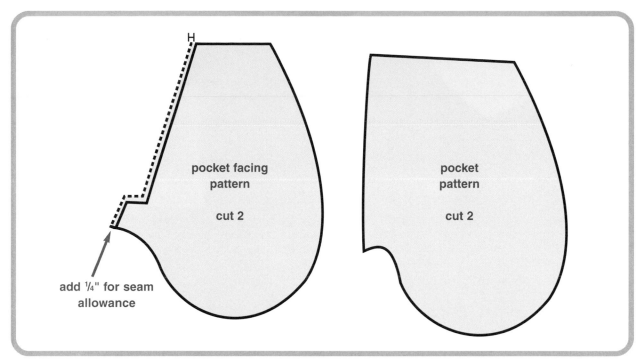

Make the pocket facing and pocket pattern.

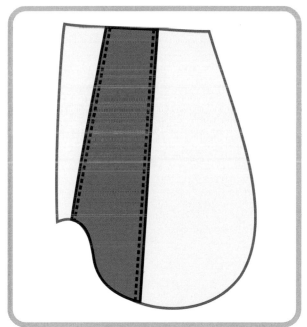

Stitch fashion fabric behind the area of the pocket opening.

2 Trace the line marking the stitching line on the inside welt piece (the stitches closest to the pant center front).

3 Make a copy of this pocket pattern. On the original pattern piece (the one with the line drawn on the welt stitches), add ¼" on the outside edge of this line for a seam allowance. Cut on this line, creating the pattern for the pocket facing.

4 Cut one pocket and one pocket facing for each pocket you are putting on your pants.

5 If you are using lining fabric for the pocket, cut an additional piece of fashion fabric large enough to cover the opening behind the welts so the fashion fabric, not lining fabric, will show through the pocket opening.

6 With right sides together, line up the pocket facing with the line of stitching on the welt closest to the center front. Stitch just shy of the original stitching line of the welt until you reach the bottom of the welts.

7 Make a ¼" clip in the pocket facing at the corner. Stitch across the bottom of the welts. Press toward the center front.

Sew the pocket facing.

Stitch the pocket facing to the inside welt piece, then press.

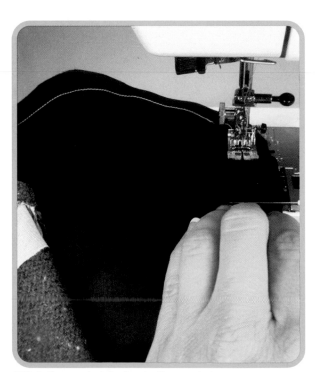

Stitch the pocket facing to the pocket.

8 Lay the pocket lining on the pocket facing with right sides together. Line up the side seam of the pant with the side seam of the pocket piece.

9 Stitch around the edges of the pocket pieces, closing the vertical opening of the pocket facing.

10 Stitch the side of the pocket to the side of the pant.

11 Serge the edges of the pocket.

12 If your pants have front pleats, fold and pin them, then trim the top of the pocket to match the top of the pant. (Transfer the shape of the top of the pocket to the original pocket pattern and you are ready to go when you make your next pair.)

13 Edgestitch or stitch in the ditch around the pocket on the top edge, the side edge, and the bottom edge. If you sew the front edge, you'll close your pocket.

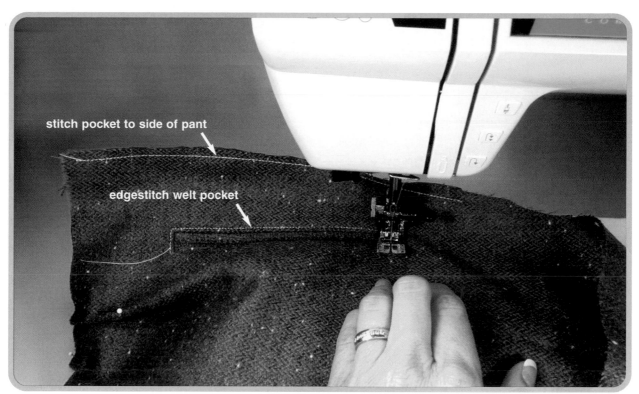

stitch pocket to side of pant

edgestitch welt pocket

Edgestitch the welt pocket.

Make the Pocket Behind the Welts for Horizontal Pockets

1 Refer to pages 54 to 56 for instructions to make the welts.

2 Make a pocket pattern as long as you desire and at least 1¼" wider than the finished pocket welts. (To find the pocket length, measure from the bottom welt to the depth of the pocket you want, turn the tape up, and measure to the top of the waist cutting line. This is usually about 14" long.)

3 If you are using lining fabric (as opposed to all fashion fabric) for the pocketing, sew a piece of fashion fabric to the top of the pocketing. The piece of fashion fabric should be long enough to cover the opening behind the welts. (Look at the back pocket on a men's pair of pants.)

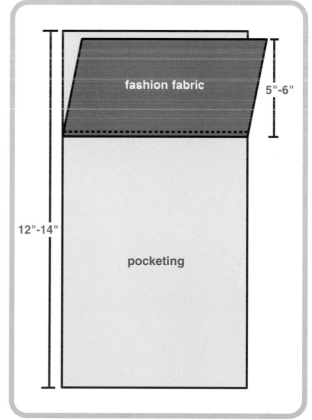

fashion fabric

5"-6"

12"-14"

pocketing

Attach the fashion fabric to the pocketing.

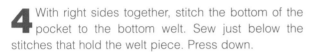

Attach the pocketing to the bottom welt.

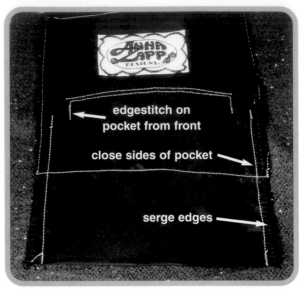

Stitch the pocket sides and edgestitch three sides of the pocket on the front.

4 With right sides together, stitch the bottom of the pocket to the bottom welt. Sew just below the stitches that hold the welt piece. Press down.

5 Fold the pocketing so the top edge meets the top of the waistline. Pin in place.

6 Stitch the pocketing to the upper welt piece the same way you did on the bottom welt piece. The top part of the pocket will be loose.

7 Stitch along the two sides of the pocket, closing the outside edges.

8 On the right side of the pants, either stitch in the ditch or edgestitch around the sides and across the top of the welt pieces.

9 If this is a jacket pocket, attach the top of the pocket first, then the bottom edge. Close the sides of the pocket as you did on the back pocket.

Stitch the pocketing to the upper welt piece.

Stitch the pocket to the top welt piece.

Close the sides of the pocket.

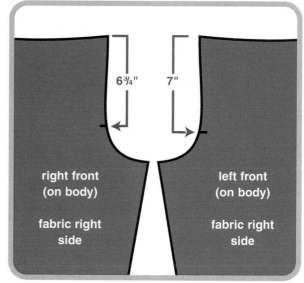

Mark the right and left zipper placements.

Faux Welt Pockets

No bulk and a good look!

1 Refer to pages 54 to 56 for instructions to make the welts.

2 Add the button loop if desired (see page 55 for instructions).

3 From the inside of the pant, sew a piece of fashion fabric all the way around the outside of the welts.

4 Stitch in the ditch or edgestitch the sides and top of the pocket.

Step 4 – Set in the Front Fly Zipper

These directions make a zipper like those on men's pants. They are for a right-handed person but if you want the fly front to face the other direction, simply reverse the facing and zipper shield sides.

When I refer to the right and left side of the pant, I am referring to the sides as if you are wearing the pants. When they are on the ironing board with the right side of the fabric facing up, they will be opposite, so always think of them as if you are wearing them.

 *Anna's Tip*

Use a zipper 9" or longer. If you use a 7" zipper, the metal stop at the top may get in your way.

1 Mark the zipper placement on the pant center front on the left side 7" from the waistline seam (longer if you are tall or need a bigger opening). Mark the right side (the zipper shield side) ¼" above the mark on the left side. My example shows 7" from the left top edge and 6¾" on the right side (on your body). At the right side mark, make a clip ⅜" deep. Don't clip the left side.

2 To make the front fly facing and zipper shield pieces, retrieve the leftover curved fabric pieces you set aside after cutting out the pant front. Refer to the illustration on page 62 and trim these pieces to have straight bottom and side edges. Cut the pieces so they are 2½" wide at the top edge. Both of these pieces are longer than necessary – you will trim them later.

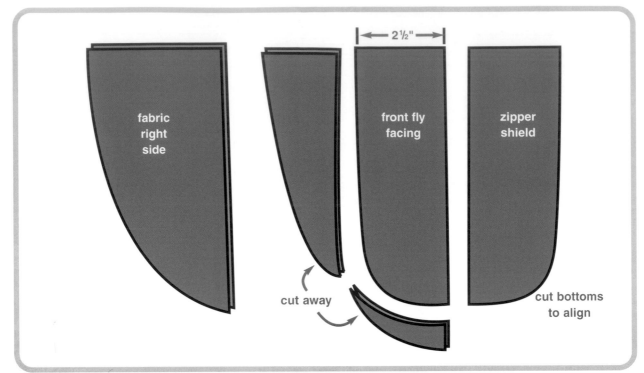

2½"

fabric
right
side

cut away

front fly
facing

zipper
shield

cut bottoms
to align

Cut the front facing and zipper shield from the leftover fabric pieces.

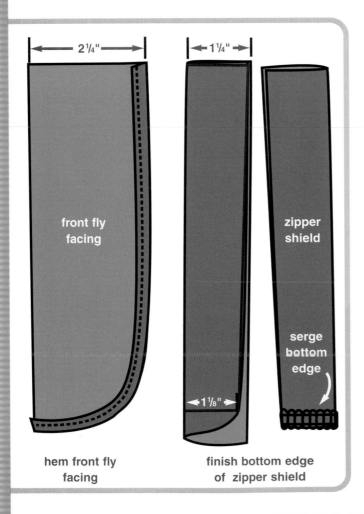

2¼"

1¼"

front fly
facing

zipper
shield

serge
bottom
edge

1⅛"

**hem front fly
facing**

**finish bottom edge
of zipper shield**

3 Hem the front facing ¼" or serge the edge. The rule is, "With the right side of the fabric facing you, the curve goes to the left." This is an easy way to remember how to hem the facing.

4 For the zipper shield, fold the other fabric piece in half with right sides together. Trim the bottom edge straight across. The bottom should be as wide as the zipper and angle to become 1¼" wide at the top. Finish the raw bottom edge by serging or zigzagging. You will finish the open side after stitching the zipper to the right center pant front.

5 Align the bottom edge of the zipper with the bottom edge of the zipper shield. Align the side edge of the zipper with the raw side edges of the zipper shield. Starting at the bottom, stitch the zipper lip through both layers of the zipper shield. You can use a regular foot with the needle in the left position. It's not necessary to stitch extremely close to the zipper teeth. Don't worry if the zipper is longer than the zipper shield at the top – you'll trim both later.

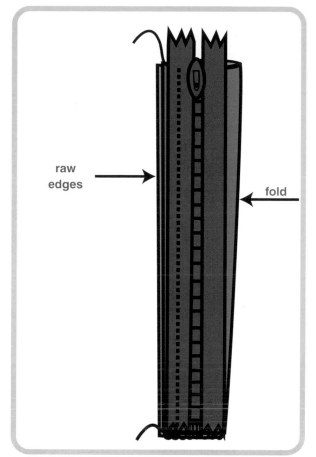

raw edges ➡ ⬅ fold

Sew the zipper to the zipper shield.

Stitch the zipper and zipper shield to the right pant front.

6 On the right pant front, fold back ⅜" from the clip to the top of the pant at the waistline and press.

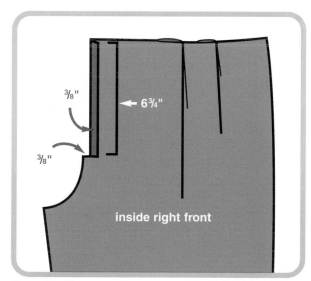

⅜"   ← 6¾"

⅜"

inside right front

Press the ⅜" seam allowance on the right side.

7 Place the zipper and zipper shield under the folded pant edge, positioning the zipper stop just above the clip. Pin and stitch along the folded edge, being careful not to place the folded edge too close to the edge of the zipper teeth. Move the zipper edge out from the folded seamline ⅛" to ¼" as you sew toward the top of the zipper/waist seamline. (This will ensure that the zipper pull will be hidden.) You can use either a regular foot or a zipper foot to stitch this area.

Anna's Tip

Since the stitching line that attaches the zipper and zipper shield to the right pant front is slightly on the bias, it may stretch about ¼", so when you sew on your waistband, you will probably have to trim this side. Don't lose sleep over this! When the time comes, just trim it off and keep going.

Stitch the front fly facing to the left side of the pants.

Understitch the front fly facing.

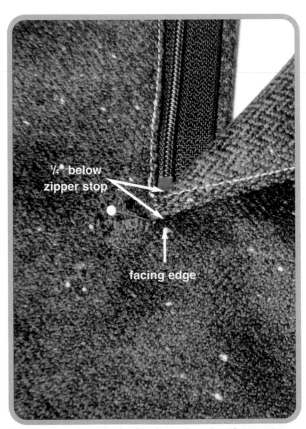

¼" below
zipper stop

facing edge

Position the front fly facing ¼" below the zipper stop.

8 Serge or zigzag stitch the seam allowance on the inside of the zipper shield.

9 Lay the facing on the left pant front with right sides together. Align it with the mark you made on the left pant front, 7" down from the waistline edge.

10 Stitch on the ⅝" seamline. Clip to the stitches and trim the seam to ¼" or grade it, trimming the seam allowance layer closest to the outside at ⅜" and the other layer to ¼".

11 Understitch, clip to the stitches, and press.

Attach the Front Pant Pieces

1 Lay both front pant pieces face up on the ironing board.

2 Position the fly facing (the left side) ¼" below the zipper stop at the bottom of the zipper. It's very important to place the facing below the zipper stop even if the right top edge ends up higher than the left. You will trim it later.

3 Position the zipper pull just below the ⅜" waistline seam. (If you are using a ⅝" seam allowance at the waistband, position the pull just below the ⅝" waistline seam.)

Position the zipper pull just below the waistline seam.

4 Position the facing edge over the zipper pull at the top and ¼" past the stitching that holds the zipper. By placing the facing on the ¼" line past the folded stitched line, the two center fronts line up and the zipper pull is safely hidden. You may notice that the right side of the zipper is a bit longer than the left. Just leave it for now.

5 Pin the faced edge to secure it. Lift the left side of the pant front and fold it so the pant fronts are right sides together, exposing the facing and the right zipper edge.

6 Fold the zipper shield out of the way and stitch the zipper edge to the facing. It doesn't matter where the stitching line is because you are only securing the zipper to the facing.

Stitch the zipper to the facing.

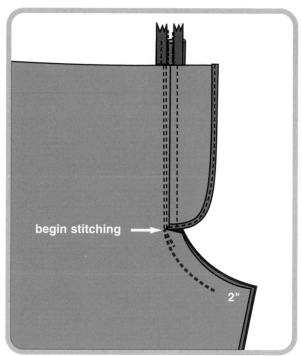

Stitch the front inseam after stitching the zipper to the facing.

7 Without moving the pieces, stitch the center (crotch) seam, beginning at the bottom of the facing stitches, backstitching, and stopping about 2" short of the inseam. Stitch through all layers, including the zipper shield.

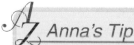
Anna's Tip

Stitching the inseam before you stitch down the fly front is the secret to a beautiful flat front fly!

8 Press the front inseam to the left with the seam allowances together. You will serge or zigzag these seams when you sew the crotch seam, after sewing the inseam.

9 Topstitch the facing to the left pant front, being sure not to catch the zipper shield at the top. (It shouldn't be in the way and it is fine to catch it at the bottom.) If you aren't used to doing this, draw a line to guide you.

10 When you reach the bottom, the facing should be ¼" lower than the metal zipper stop. Stitch below it, catching all the layers. Turn and stitch up a couple of stitches to close this area. Turn again and stitch back to the bottom stitch line, creating secure stitches in the shape of a triangle.

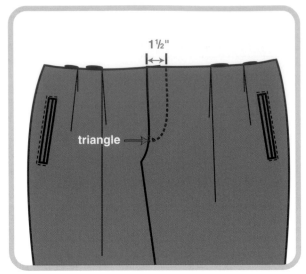

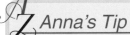

Topstitch the front fly, making a triangle at the bottom.

It's very important to pin the top of the zipper before cutting it even with the waist.

11 I know you are dying to cut off the zipper and zipper shield! Unzip the zipper and insert a straight pin or safety pin across the zipper on one side. After pinning the zipper, you can cut off the excess. (I can't tell you how many times I've seen the zipper pull lost because the zipper wasn't pinned.)

12 Secure the pleat folds *only* across the waistband seamline. You will permanently set the pleats later, after you finish the pants and know where you want them to fall over your tummy.

Step 5 – Mark and Partially Sew the Pants Back

1 If you haven't already done so, mark the center back seam as it is not the same width all the way up.

2 Stitch the darts and make the welt pockets on the back if desired (see pages 54 to 56 for welt pocket instructions).

3 Sew the center back seam, starting about 2" from the inseam and stopping where the seam begins to widen. You will serge this seam and the front crotch seam later.

Step 6 – Attach the Front and Back Pieces

1 Serge or zigzag the edges of the side seams and inseams.

2 Sew the side seams on the 1" seam allowance (or whatever seam allowance you are using). Press the seams open.

3 Start stitching the inseam ⅝" below the top of the inseam. Press or topstitch the front crotch seam facing the left. Press the back crotch seam open.

Anna's Tip

If you are not sure of the fit of the pants, baste the side seams and the inseams.

Anna's Tip

When matching the inseam to the side seams, make sure the front and back pieces move straight across each other. *Don't force the hemline or crotch line to meet.* If you force the hem or crotch lengths to meet and the pieces don't slide straight across one another, you will end up with the dreaded twist in the leg. If the pieces don't slide straight across, slide them straight across and trim the edges to meet, whether at the crotch seamline or the hemline. Remember to adjust your pattern for the next pair.

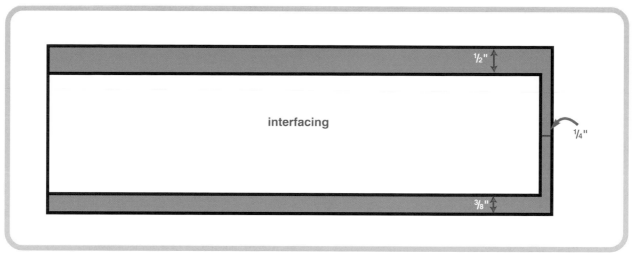

Fuse interfacing to the left waistband.

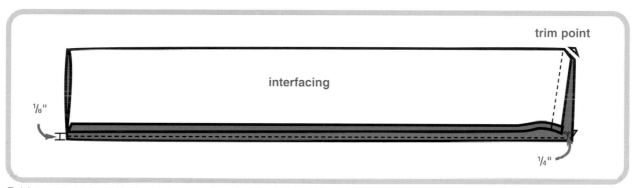

Fold, press, and stitch the bottom and end of the left waistband.

4 Press the inseams open. Sew the remaining open area of the crotch seamline (about 4"). The top of the inseam will be open the ⅝" you didn't stitch. Don't serge or finish this seam yet. You'll do that when you sew the center back seam after the final fitting.

5 Press the side seams either open or together. If you press them together, press them toward the front (this is opposite of what manufacturers do). This gives a cleaner look from the front.

Step 7 – Interface and Sew the Waistband Pieces

1 Start with the left waistband (the side with the front fly facing). Cut interfacing for the waistband twice the width of the finished waistband plus ⅛" and as long as the pattern piece for the left waistband.

2 Place the interfacing on the fabric waistband so the fabric extends ⅜" beyond the bottom edge of the interfacing, ½" on the top, and ¼" on the right end. Fuse the interfacing to the fabric.

3 Fold the top and bottom fabric over the interfacing and press.

4 Fold the waistband piece lengthwise, leaving an extension of ⅛" on the bottom edge. Press, then stitch the bottom edge. Sew the right end and trim the point.

5 Turn inside out and push out the corner for a nice clean point. (I use a small Phillips head screwdriver.) You should have a clean edge with no bulk from the seam.

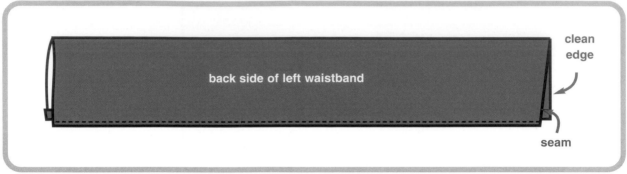

Fuse interfacing to the left waistband. Fold, press, and stitch the bottom and end of the left waistband.

Hem the back side.

6 Fuse interfacing end to end on the right waistband fabric piece (the side with the zipper shield).

7 Fold in half lengthwise with wrong sides together. Press, then hem the bottom edge of the back side.

Anna's Tip

To help set the fold, lay some weights on the fold after pressing and let the piece cool before handling it.

Step 8 – Check the Fit

If you are not sure of the fit of the pants, pin or baste on the waistband, pin the center back closed, and check the fit. (To do a really good fitting, the waistband must be in place.)

1 If the crotch is too high, remember that it will move away from your body (drop) with wear. If you love the way it fits, stitch twill tape or a narrow tape that is on the straight of grain in the seamline in the curved area (about midway up from the inseam). This will prevent the crotch seam from stretching, which it would normally do because the curve is on the bias.

2 If the crotch is too low, pull the pants up and mark where the waistband should sit. This is about the only way to remedy this problem. The inseam may be taken in a bit to raise the crotch slightly.

3 Check the general fit of the pants. Make sure the side seams are in the middle of your body.

4 Check the fullness. Sit down and check how the inseams feel.

5 If the center back seam is deeper than you planned, you can reposition the back pieces. If the darts are in the right place, simply cut off the excess seam allowance at the center back. The seam allowance should be 1½" to 1¾" deep.

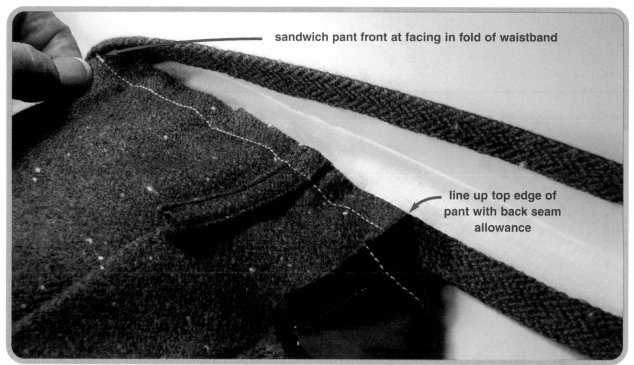

sandwich pant front at facing in fold of waistband

line up top edge of pant with back seam allowance

Insert the left pant front into the waistband.

Step 9 – Attach the Waistband

Left Waistband

1 If your pant pattern has a ⅝" seam allowance, trim the waistline seam to ⅜". Mark this seamline with a marker or by staystitching.

2 Pin the belt loops in place or stitch them as you staystitch.

3 Sandwich the left pant center front between the two pressed edges of the waistband, placing the front edge of the front fly facing exactly flush and inside the fold of the waistband. Pin in place. *Note: When you stitch on the waistband, the top edge of the pants will line up exactly with the top edge of the folded waistband edge.*

4 Begin stitching at the center front. Put the needle down exactly where you want the waistband to be attached, make a couple of forward stitches then a couple of backward stitches, then sew on the waistband, edgestitching through all thicknesses. Because you catch the back side of the waistband when you stitch the front, there will only be one row of stitching.

5 Stitch until you reach the back dart or the end of the belt loop on the back piece.

inside left side

seamline

one row of stitching catches front and back of waistband

Stitch the left side of the waistband to the pant front.

right side of pants

Open the waistband after backstitching over the belt loop.

6 Backstitch across the belt loop and put the needle in the down position. Lift the presser foot and pull the underside of the waistband out of the way of the needle.

7 Pick up the needle and move the waistband forward, skipping over the backstitching you just did. Continue stitching the waistband, catching only the waistband and the pant fabric until you reach the end of that side of the pant.

8 Turn the waistband over and clip the stitch to release the fold in the waistband.

Anna's Tip

If you find this difficult or confusing, stop sewing and move the underside of the waistband out of the way and stitch only the top layer of the waistband to the center back.

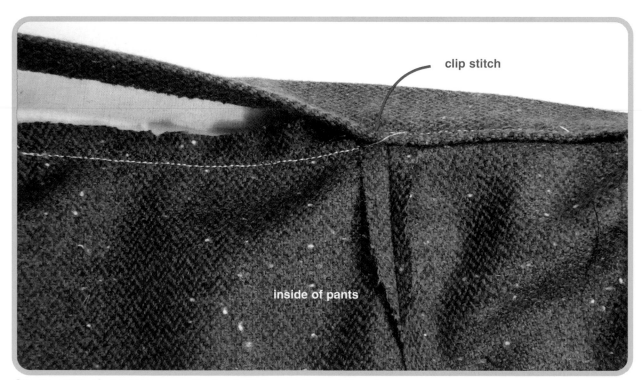

clip stitch

inside of pants

Clip the stitch after skipping over the backstitches on the waistband.

Stitch the right front band at the center back, catching only one layer of the waistband and the pant at the waistline.

Right Waistband

1 Begin at the center back. With the waistband open, edgestitch the waistband (front layer only) and pant back until you reach the back dart or the belt loop.

2 Stop stitching and fold the waistband so you will catch all the layers.

right back of pant

Stitch the waistband past the back belt loop.

3 Stitch to the zipper shield, making sure both sides of the waistband line up at the top of the zipper.

4 Trim the excess waistband at the zipper shield and finish the raw edge. If you prefer, you can leave this a bit longer (1½" or so) and add a buttonhole to be buttoned to the inside of the waistband. (I like to finish this raw edge by zigzagging twice because that produces the least bulk.) If you serge the edge, tie off the thread ends.

5 Add a waistband closure (hook and eye or button and buttonhole).

Finish the right side of the waistband at the zipper shield.

Leave a wide seam allowance at the center back.

Step 10 – Finish the Center Back Seam

1 Try on your pants. *Sit down* and mark the center back seam at the waistline. This may or may not be exactly where it is on your pattern, but it will be the correct place for the finished seamline.

2 Begin stitching at the seamline where you left off when stitching the center back seam.

3 Stitch the center back seam, angling the seamline toward the finished mark at the center back seamline. The seam allowance will get deeper as you move to the top.

4 Leave the center back seam allowance about 1½" deep so you can change the waistband size if necessary. (I let out and take in the back center seam as my waistline fluctuates!)

5 After sewing the center seam all the way up the center back, press the seams open. Serge the center back seams and trim the seam to ⅜" where the curve is the deepest. Press open. The seams tend to spread apart so leave the seam open ⅝" from the top.

6 Serge the front crotch seam. Trim the seam to ⅜" and press it to the left (the way it wants to go). You may want to edgestitch the seam from the front.

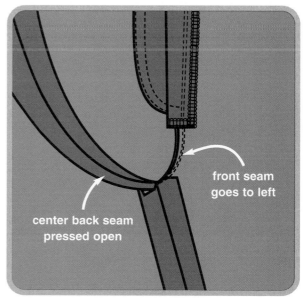

front seam goes to left

center back seam pressed open

Finish the inside crotch seam intersection.

Step 11 – Attach the Belt Loops

1 Serge or zigzag the top edge of the belt loops. Trim the corners.

2 Align the top of the belt loops with the top of the waistband and stitch.

Step 12 – Set the Pleats and Hem the Pants

When pleats are pressed in manufacturing and dry cleaning, the pants are put on an ironing board or in a pressing machine that presses the pleats on a flat surface. Consequently, when you wear the pants, the pleats open up because they were pressed on a flat surface and we are not flat across our tummies. If you have spent time pressing the pleats in the right place, ask the dry cleaner to follow your pressing lines. Many times, I have had to re-press the area of my pleats between my waist and mid-thigh to get them to lay flat across my tummy. It's not that the pants don't fit (or that you've gained weight since you took the pants to the cleaners!) it's that the pleats weren't pressed correctly.

Most sewers think pleats make them look larger. This is because the pleats weren't pressed correctly. If your pleats are set correctly in the first place, they will not open – they will lay flat and look great.

1 Lay the right leg of the pants on the ironing board. Move the left leg up and out of the way.

2 Line up the inseam and the side seam at the crotch line and at the hemline. (The front should already have a soft crease in it.)

Anna's Tip

Set the pleats with the pants *on your body*. You can't set pleats on the ironing board because it is flat and if you use a mitt or ham, you will have to guess at the amount of curve you have at your tummy.

3 Press the front and back creases, stopping at the crotch seam. Repeat with the left leg.

4 Try on the pants and pin the pleats where they want to fall over your tummy. (You may want to top-stitch the pleats in place or stitch under the first pleat, catching the pocket to secure the pleat.)

5 Mark the hem on the pant legs.

Anna's Tip

When you hang pants, I have found that if you unzip the zipper and fold the waistband at the first pleat or dart, they hang much flatter. This also works well when packing them.

6 On the ironing board, press the pinned pleats using a pressing mitt if necessary. Since bodies are not flat, there will be a slight curve to the pleats.

7 The front crease, pressed up to the crotch line, should line up with the lower edge of the pleat at the waistline. If the pleat curves over your tummy, the fold of the pleat may be slightly curved.

8 Hem the pant legs by hand or with a blind stitch on the machine.

Chapter 4

Sew Easy Lined Vests, Camisoles & Sleeveless Tops

The techniques in this chapter can be used to make a lined vest, camisole, sleeveless shell, and even a cap-sleeved blouse. This simple method will help you create a professionally finished garment that can be easily altered and can be made reversible.

This chapter combines two garments – a vest and camisole – that are constructed the same way except that the vest has two front pieces and the camisole has one.

These garments are perfect for embroidery or appliqué. If you think the fabric for the vest front needs extra body, fuse interfacing to it before embroidering. Depending on the embroidery or appliqué design, it's usually best to do the embellishment before cutting the pattern pieces. If you embroider the garment after it's finished, you'll have to stitch through all the layers and the stitching will show on the inside.

Even though the garments can be made reversible, in these instructions I refer to the outside pieces as the fashion fabric and the inside pieces as the lining fabric.

Before beginning, refer to Chapter 1 to measure and adjust your pattern. If you are still unsure of the fit, cut and baste the front and back pieces together (or cut the pieces out of muslin) and check the fit. Make any changes to the garment and transfer them to the pattern.

The embroidery design "Ribbons and Roses" is from my embroidery disk Western Appliqué for Amazing Designs.

The embroidery design "Alpine Blue Columbine" is from my disk, Rocky Mountain High, Signature #55, for Cactus Punch.

Step 1 – Prepare the Fabric and Cut Out the Garment

1 For a vest, consider using a heavier weight fabric for the front and a lighter weight for the back. Depending on the fabric, fuse interfacing on all the pieces or on only the front pieces. The fabric in the sample vest is nubby silk so I fused fusible tricot on all the vest pieces. The interfacing adds body and makes for a more crisp, tailored look. Any type of fusible tricot can be used on many lightweight fabrics to add enough body to make a nice vest. **Note:** *If the fabric is really lightweight, be careful that the fuse dots don't show through the fabric.*

Apply the fusible interfacing to the fabric before cutting the pieces. Be sure to use the right type of fusible interfacing for the fabric. If in doubt, do a test by fusing different types to scraps of your fabric and letting them cool before making your decision.

2 Cut out the garment and lining pieces. If you are making a reversible garment, the lining can be the same type of fabric in a different color or design. Just be sure the lining doesn't show through the fashion fabric.

Note. In the photos the lining is darker than the garment so you can clearly distinguish between the lining and fashion fabric and so you can see the understitching. I wouldn't normally put a dark lining behind a light fashion fabric.

3 Sew any darts or seams in the vest or camisole front pieces of the fashion fabric.

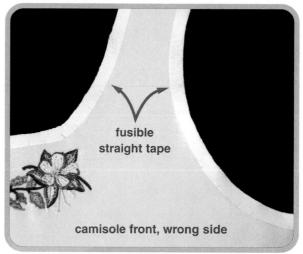

Apply fusible straight tape to the neckline and armholes of the camisole. Make clips in the tape at the curved areas.

Step 2 - Interface and Stabilize the Edges

The instructions for your vest pattern may instruct you to add interfacing along the front edge or on the front facing, especially if there will be buttonholes and buttons. Apply the interfacing to either the facing or to the front and/or bottom edges. Even if you interfaced the entire garment with a light fusible, you may still need additional interfacing on the front and bottom edges. Your pattern will probably include facing pattern pieces and tell you to use the pattern pieces for the facing as well as the interfacing. (If there's no closure on the vest you may not need to interface these areas.) If you like a lot of structure, interface along the front and bottom of the vest edges, the back neckline, and the armholes. If you interface these places, you may not need to do the following steps.

1 To stabilize the edges with ⅜" wide fusible straight tape, trim the seam allowances of the camisole neckline and armholes (front and back) to ¼". Trim the seam allowances of the vest front and bottom edge, neckline, and armholes to ¼". Trim the seam allowances of the lining pieces as you did on the garment fronts and backs.

2 Measure and cut the lengths of tape you need in each area. Apply the tape to the wrong side of the fabric on top of the interfacing.

3 For the vest, fuse tape to the edges of the neckline, armholes, and front and bottom edges. For the camisole, fuse tape to the edges of the neckline and armholes. Make ⅛" deep clips in the tape about ⅜" apart on all the curved areas. The tape will hold the shape of these curved areas through many washings and wearings.

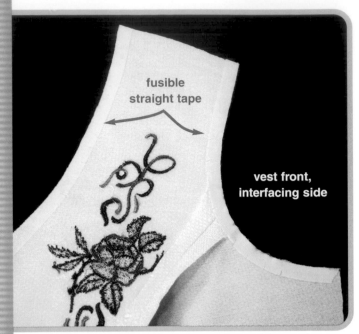

Apply fusible straight tape to the neckline and armholes of the vest. Make clips in the tape at the curved areas.

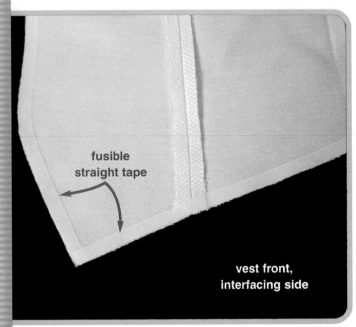

Apply fusible straight tape to the front and bottom edges of the vest.

4 **To stabilize the edges with ¼" twill tape,** don't trim any seam allowances and proceed with the construction. You will apply the tape in Step 3.

Step 3 – Make the Front Pieces

1 Attach any pockets or decoration not already applied. I embroidered my vest front before I sewed the pieces together.

2 If your pattern calls for a front facing, sew the front facing to the front lining piece(s) after it has been interfaced. If you prefer not to use the facing piece, cut the lining pieces the same as you did the fashion fabric and sew them the same way as the vest or camisole front. (Additional pieces apply to a vest or camisole with French seams.)

3 If you are using twill tape to reinforce the armholes and necklines, center the twill tape on the seamlines and sew through all the layers. Trim the seamlines to ¼" and clip to the stitching line. (Be careful – it's no fun when you clip through your stitch!)

4 Sew the lining to the vest or camisole. On the vest, with right sides together, stitch the lining to the fashion fabric along the front and bottom edge on the seamline. On the camisole, stitch the lining to the fashion fabric along the neckline of the front piece only.

5 Finish this seamline in one of these ways:

- Press the seam allowances toward the lining. From the right side, press and edgestitch.
- Clip the curves and understitch the areas you just stitched (the neckline of the camisole and the bottom and front edge of the vest). If your vest has corners along the bottom edge, understitch as far as you can to the corner, backstitch, pick up the needle, and continue understitching as close to the corner as possible. If your vest has a curved edge,

Anna's Tip

To understitch, fold both seam allowances toward the lining and stitch very close to the seam edge from the *right* side of the garment, edgestitching on the lining side. Pull the fabric flat. If your piece is reversible, evenly understitch close to the edge of one side (usually the darker side). This will look like edgestitching on that side and show a clean finish on the other side. If your vest or camisole is not reversible, understitching is the only way to go.

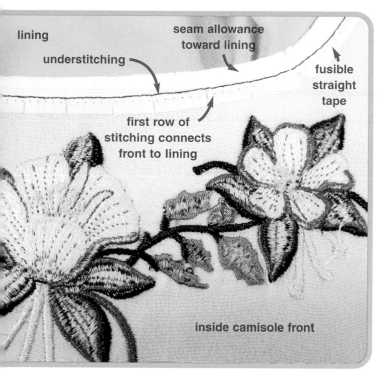

lining

understitching

seam allowance toward lining

fusible straight tape

first row of stitching connects front to lining

inside camisole front

Understitch from the inside of the camisole.

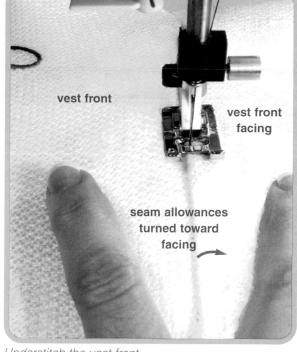

vest front

vest front facing

seam allowances turned toward facing

Understitch the vest front.

you should be able to understitch the entire bottom edge. Sometimes it is easier to understitch with the garment turned inside out.

■ On the camisole only, press the seam allowances toward the lining. From the right side, press and edgestitch. Press with one side rolling out about ¹⁄₁₆", creating the look of a tiny piping. (I once sent very expensive reversible camisoles to a store in Hawaii and they thought I had made them with tiny piping!) If you like this idea, it's easiest to roll out the side with the twill tape or fused straight tape.

6 Press flat the edges of the neckline on the camisole and the vest front and bottom edges. Line up the armholes, bottom edge (camisole), and side seams. Trim the lining and the fashion fabric to exactly the same size. The shoulder seam, armholes, side seams, and bottom edge of the camisole are still open, as are the armholes, shoulder seam, and side seams on the front vest pieces.

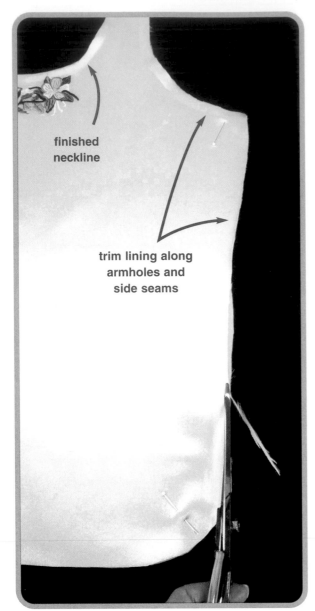

finished
neckline

trim lining along
armholes and
side seams

Trim the camisole lining to match the fashion fabric.

Trim the vest lining after stitching it to the front and understitching the front and lower edge.

7 Turn the piece/pieces so the right sides are facing. For the vest, stitch the armholes and finish the seams the same way you did for the vest front and bottom edge. With wider straps, you will be able to understitch the entire length of the strap. For the camisole, stitch the armholes and across the bottom edge. Understitch as far as you can.

8 Turn the garment inside out and press all the edges. The camisole side seams and shoulder seams are still open.

Step 4 – Connect the Back and Back Lining to the Front

If you are making a camisole, first read the vest instructions.

Vest

1 Prepare the neckline and armholes of the back piece with fusible straight tape or twill tape just as you did on the front pieces.

2 Sew any darts or seams in the vest back and lining.

3 Lay the lining back piece right side up on the cutting table. Lay the front pieces right side up on top of the lining.

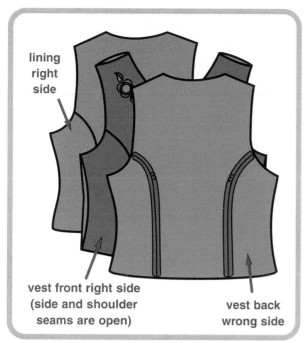

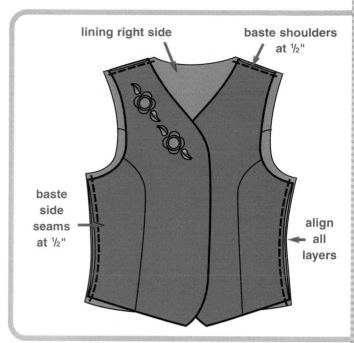

Layer the pieces as shown.

Baste the shoulder and side seams.

4 Align the side seam edges, shoulder seam edges, and the back neck edge. Pin in place.

5 Baste the side seams and shoulder seams on the ½" seamline.

6 Pin the vest back and front with right sides together.

7 Begin stitching at the lower left edge, catching all the layers until you reach the top of the armhole of the front piece.

8 Put your needle in the down position, pivot, and sew the back armhole, catching only the armhole lining and fashion fabric layers. Don't catch the front armhole.

9 Stop stitching when you reach the top of the armhole at the shoulder. Put your needle in the down position, pivot, and sew across all the layers of the shoulder, stopping when you reach the end of the shoulder front.

10 With the needle in the down position, pivot and stitch across the back neckline until you reach the other shoulder seam. Put the needle down, pivot, and stitch across the shoulder. Continue stitching this side the same way you did on the first side, finishing at the bottom edge of the lining and fashion fabric.

Stitch the lining and back pieces to the vest fronts.

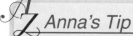 **Anna's Tip**

When pivoting at the armhole and shoulder corners, put the needle down exactly past the front finished edges. If you stitch too far or not far enough at the pivot points of the armhole or neckline areas, you will have a problem when you turn it inside out.

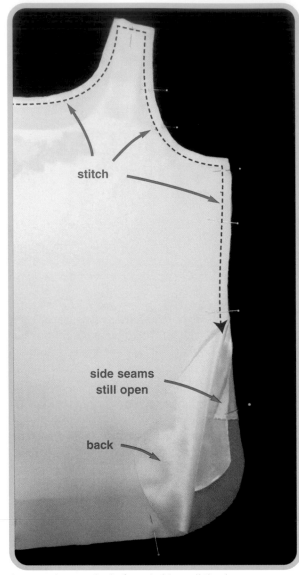

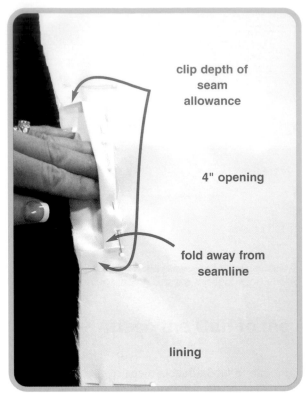

clip depth of
seam
allowance

4" opening

fold away from
seamline

lining

Clip the lining to form an opening for turning.

stitch

side seams
still open

back

Lay up the camisole for stitching all the layers.

Camisole

1 Prepare the neckline and armholes of the back piece with fusible straight tape or twill tape as you did on the front pieces.

2 Lay up the camisole pieces in the same order as the vest – lining face up, front face up, then the back face down. Pin through all the layers. As you can see in the photo, my pattern has a curved hem and a place to stop stitching on the side seam.

3 Make two clips the depth of your seam allowance about 4" apart along the lining on the side seam and fold it out of the way of the seamline. This creates an opening so you can turn the camisole inside out.

4 Stitch around all the edges, side seams, across the shoulder, back neck edge, and armhole. ***Note:*** *When stitching the side seams at the opening, fold the lining out of the way and don't catch it in the stitching.*

5 Understitch the neckline and the armholes (or finish as desired). The back hemline is still open.

6 With right sides together, stitch the camisole back across the back hemline.

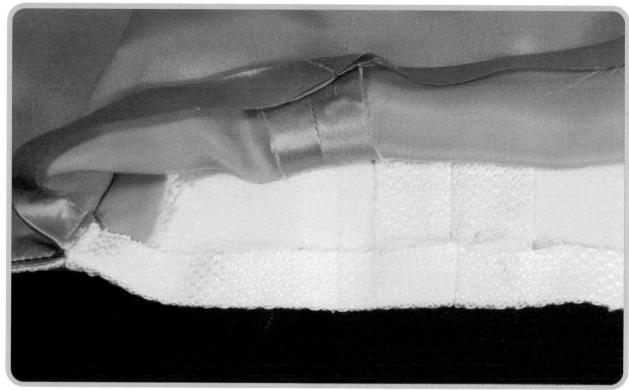

Press the seam allowance on the back hem.

Step 5 – Finish the Garment

Vest

1 Turn the vest inside out through the bottom back edge. Reach inside and understitch the armhole and back neckline seams of the back piece. When understitching, sew as far as you can in the space you have. Press all the edges.

2 Hang the garment and align the back piece with the lining. On both the lining and the back piece, press under ⅝" (or the amount of the seam allowance) toward the inside and edgestitch or slipstitch all the way across the back bottom edge. Press.

3 To close, edgestitch along the hemline on the back of the vest.

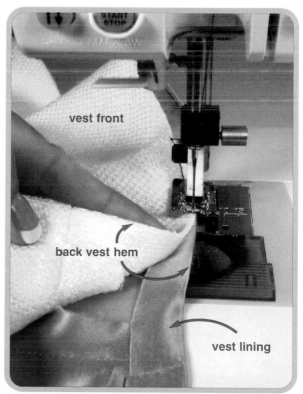

vest front

back vest hem

vest lining

Stitch the lining and vest back closed at the hemline.

Photo by Mellisa K. Mahoney

The tailoring methods in this chapter can also be used to make a double-breasted vest. This white vest is made of serged rayon with cut shell buttons.

Camisole

1 Turn the camisole right side out through the opening. Press

2 Hand stitch the opening closed or fold it back exactly on the seamline stitches and machine stitch it closed. Press.

3 Hand roll the back hemline seam flat and press. You probably won't be able to understitch the back hemline seam.

Chapter 5

Create Beautiful Tailored Shirts

*The first western shirt I sewed took me 18 hours and I got paid $8 for it in 1971. Part of the problem was that the fabric had no right and wrong sides and I made two right arm sleeves, which I didn't notice until it was finished, **double** topstitched, pressed, and ready for snaps! The owner of the store made me rip it all out and re-sew the sleeve, vent, and cuff. I didn't give up, though, and I never made that mistake again. When I was making custom western shirts for a living, I could sew three shirts in a day. I had the construction down to a fine science and that is what you will learn in this chapter.*

You can use the tailoring methods in this chapter with any commercial pattern. The instructions here are for women's shirts and are set up so that you can do "no-think" sewing. This is a no-frills, get-it-done-and-on way to make a shirt. Once you have perfected the fit, you will fly through the construction.

Be creative with your shirt. Choose one fabric for the body and another for the front bands, back yoke, or cuffs and sleeve vents. Mix solids and prints, prints and prints, solids and solids, etc. Embellish with embroidery and/or appliqué designs.

Step 1 – Prepare the Pattern

1 Choose a commercial pattern that has a collar band (or collar stand). Set aside the pattern piece for the collar band.

2 Refer to your Measurement Chart (pages 10 to 13) and compare your measurements to those of the commercial pattern pieces. Adjust the pattern pieces using the methods you learned in Chapter 1. If you are uncertain about the length of the sleeve or shirt, add extra length. The first time you sew your revised pattern, you will put in the sleeves before you add the cuff. That way, you can fit the sleeve length then transfer any changes to the pattern so the next time you sew the shirt, it will be just right.

3 Change the ⅝" seam allowances of the following pattern pieces to ⅜" by trimming off ¼":

- collar
- cuff
- shoulder
- yoke
- sleeve cap
- armhole

Note: After you fit the sleeve length on the first sewing, you will trim the seam allowance of the lower sleeve edge (where the cuff attaches) to ⅜", but not until you are sure of your sleeve length.

4 Leave the sleeve seam and the side seams at ⅝". This is a good size seam allowance in case you need to let the shirt out.

5 Most commercial shirt patterns come with a right front and a left front. Choose one and discard the other. (It doesn't make any difference which one you keep.) On this front piece define the center line and draw a line 1" from the center line, toward the outside. Cut along the line you just drew, trimming off any remaining part of the pattern front. This is your new cutting line for the two fronts.

Anna's Tip

If you like French seams, flat-felled seams, or any other seam finishes, adjust the seam allowances to achieve the finish you want.

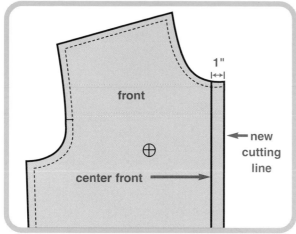

Draw the new cutting line 1" from the center line.

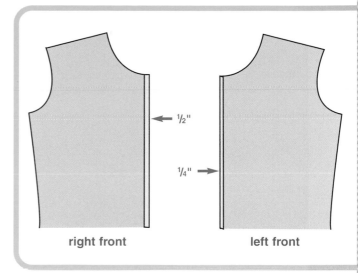

Turn back the shirt front edges.

6 Make a new front band pattern piece 2¼" wide and 1" longer than the length of the shirt front piece. I usually position the shirt front about 3" from the selvage edge and cut the front band piece between the shirt front edge and the selvage edge. Or you can measure and draw on the fabric just beyond the shirt front edge.

Step 2 – Cut Out the Shirt and Interfacing

Interfacing is critical for making a shirt look tailored. Choose a stiff, good quality interfacing for the collar and cuffs. You may think the interfacing is too stiff, but after a few washings, it will lose quite a bit of body, so don't be afraid to buy a good stiff interfacing.

For cotton, cotton blends, linens, silk broadcloth, or similar materials, I suggest Veriform. If you have a very soft, lightweight fabric, add fusible interfacing to the upper cuff to give it more body.

1 After preparing the pattern pieces, pin them on fabric, lining up the grain lines as the shown on the pattern. Cut all the pieces except the collar band from fabric. (You will cut the collar band in Step 5.)

2 Cut interfacing pieces for the collar and cuff, the same size as the pattern pieces.

3 From interfacing, cut a right front band 1¼" wide and a left front band ⅞" wide, each 1" longer than the shirt front.

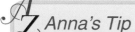 *Anna's Tip*

When making a man's shirt, reverse the front bands. The 1¼" band goes on the left shirt front and the ⅞" band goes on the right shirt front.

Step 3 – Sew the Front Bands and Pockets

1 With the right sides of the shirt fronts facing up, turn back ½" on the right front and ¼" on the left front, causing the right side of the fabric to fold back on itself (right side closure). Press.

2 On the right front band, fold the front band fabric piece around the interfacing strip lengthwise and press, making it the same size as the interfacing.

3 On the left front band, fold the front band strip over the interfacing edge and press. If the fabric edges overlap, trim the shirt band fabric so that it just touches, not overlaps. (You could have trimmed this piece before pressing it, but then you would have had to think about it when you cut your front band strips. Do it however you like.)

4 To attach the right front band, turn the shirt so the hemline is at the top and the wrong side of the fabric is facing up. Place the front band under the shirt front and extend the folded edge of the front band ¼" past the folded edge of the shirt front. With the right side of the front band facing down, stitch on the edge of the shirt fold. When you look at the right side of the shirt, the topstitching should be ¼" from the edge of the front band. (Make sure your bobbin stitch is pretty.) This can also be stitched from the front side, but it's trickier.

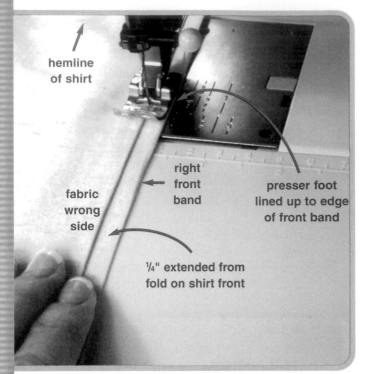

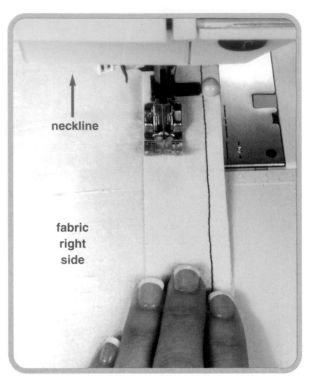

With the shirt front wrong side up, stitch the right front band to the shirt, starting at the hem.

Topstitch the right side of the front band from the neckline of the shirt.

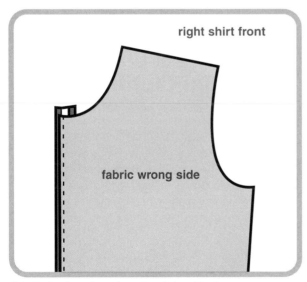

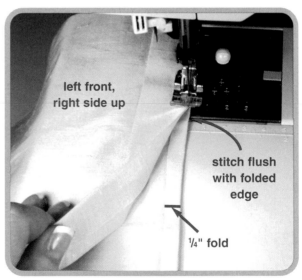

Stitch the front band on the right shirt front.

Stitch the left front band flush with the folded shirt edge.

5 Turn the shirt so the front is right side up and stitch ¼" from the remaining folded edge of the front band. Trim the front band even with the shirt at the neckline or the hemline.

6 Place the folded, pressed edge of the left front band flush with the folded edge of the left shirt front. (The raw edge of the shirt fold will be under the front band.) With the right side up, edgestitch the outer edge of the left front band, then edgestitch the remaining edge of the left front band. Trim the front bands even with the neckline and the hem of the shirt.

7 Add pockets if desired. If you are adding one on each side, measure from the center of both front bands for correct placement. You can also pin the front closed, matching the front bands at the center of each band and then measure the pocket placement.

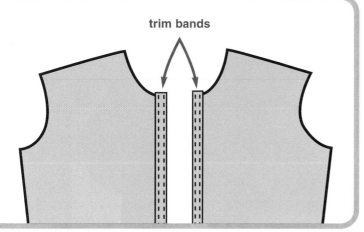

The finished fronts before adding pockets.

Step 4 – Sew the Back Yoke and Shoulder Seam

1 Pin or stitch any tucks in the shirt back.

2 With right sides together, sandwich the shirt back between the yoke and the yoke lining pieces (these may be the same fabric). The right side of the yoke lining should face the wrong side of the shirt. Straight stitch with a ⅜" seam allowance through all the layers, all the way across.

3 Press the yoke and yoke lining so they face up toward the neckline, then edgestitch or topstitch along the yoke seamline.

4 With the right side of the yoke lining to the wrong side of the shirt fabric, straight stitch the shirt to the yoke lining at the shoulders, using a ⅜" seam allowance. Press the seam allowance to the back.

5 Lay the folded shoulder yoke edge over the line of stitching, connecting the shirt front and back yoke lining, and edgestitch through all the layers.

shirt back

fabric right side

Sandwich the shirt back between the yoke and yoke lining.

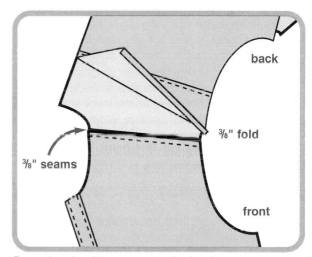

back

⅜" fold

⅜" seams

front

Press the shoulder seams to the back.

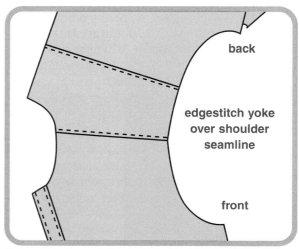

back

edgestitch yoke over shoulder seamline

front

Edgestitch the yoke over the shoulder seam.

Step 5 – Adjust the Collar Band Pattern

One of the hardest parts of putting on a collar band is fitting it to the neckline. With experience I learned that the collar band should be ¼" to ⅜" longer than the opening of the neckline. A neckline that is "kind of" gathered into the collar band is a dead give-away that it is not a professional job.

The collar band has an "upper" piece and an "under" piece. The upper collar band is the piece that touches your neck and the under collar band is the piece that's under the collar when the collar is folded down. Commercial patterns usually only have one pattern piece for the collar band but you cut two of that piece. The terms "upper" and "under" are correct for the collar band pieces and that's how I refer to them in the following instructions.

1 Retrieve the collar band pattern piece you set aside and trim the seam allowances to ⅜". Measure your neck circumference and the length of the collar band pattern. If the collar band isn't a bit longer than your neck circumference, either lengthen the collar band (remember to lengthen the collar pattern piece by the same amount) or make the neckline opening smaller by taking some off the shoulder seamline. The neckline is on the bias and will stretch just enough to fit beautifully if the collar band is slightly longer. If the neckline opening is too large, you will have a hard time. Most people don't button the top button on the collar band, but the collar band should still be close to your neck size. The collar band and collar will shrink with laundering, so it's wise to cut both pieces ¼" longer than your neck size.

2 After you've adjusted the collar band pattern, cut it out of fabric and interfacing.

Step 6 – Sew the Collar

In these instructions, the "upper" collar refers to the part of the collar you see when you're wearing the shirt and the "under" collar is the piece underneath. Again, your commercial pattern will probably have one collar pattern piece and instruct you to cut two.

1 Pin the interfacing to the wrong side of the upper collar fabric piece. Stitch the lower neck edge at ⅛" to secure and pin the remaining edges (you may also stitch them at ⅛").

2 *Optional:* Because the collar curves, the inside curve is a bit smaller than the outside, so you may want to cut the under collar piece ⅛" shorter than the upper collar and interfacing. Even if you don't do this, you will still have a beautiful collar.

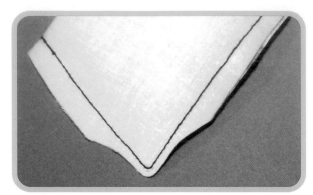

Trim the seam around the point on the collar.

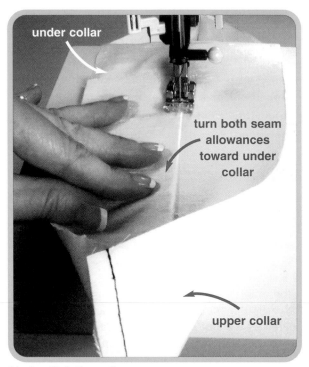

under collar

turn both seam allowances toward under collar

upper collar

Understitch the collar.

3 Pin the collar pieces right sides together and stitch the collar with the interfacing on the top. If you cut the under collar smaller, pull it gently so that all the edges match. This will create the slightest curve in the collar around your neck.

4 Instead of stitching a sharp corner at the collar point, make one stitch across the point and trim around the point as pictured. Don't turn it right side out yet.

5 With the seam facing the under collar, understitch the under collar from the right side as far as you can stitch.

6 Turn the collar right side out and push out the collar points. (The points may be slightly square.)

7 Press and edgestitch or topstitch the collar around the three outer edges you just sewed.

Step 7 – Attach the Collar to the Collar Band

1 Stitch the interfacing to the wrong side of the upper collar band piece ⅛" from the neck edge.

2 Fold the lower edge of the upper collar band under ⅜" and press.

3 Sandwich the collar between the collar band pieces. The upper collar and upper collar band (the interfaced piece) should be right sides together, as should the under collar and the under collar band.

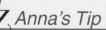
Anna's Tip

If your fabric is hard to handle, stitch ¼" from the lower folded edge of the collar band to secure the fold.

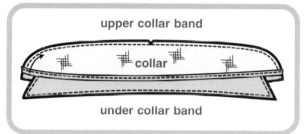

Sandwich the collar between the upper and under collar bands.

4 Begin stitching at one end of the collar band and stitch all the way to the other end. The ⅜" seam allowance of the under collar band will hang below the upper collar band.

5 Check to make sure the curves are the same at both ends of the collar band. Trim the collar band seam at the curve to ⅛".

6 Understitch the seam to the under collar very close to the seam edge.

7 Fold the collar at the collar band and press. Pin the collar and collar band around a pressing ham and steam it to set the folds.

Place the collar and collar band on a pressing ham.

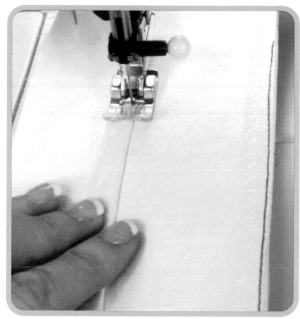

Understitch the collar band.

Note the professional look of this neckline.

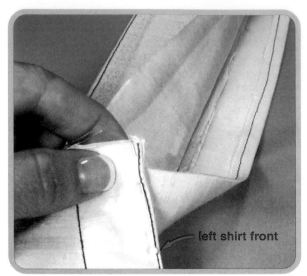

Pin the under collar to the neckline at the left front.

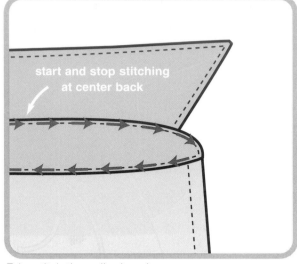

Edgestitch the collar band.

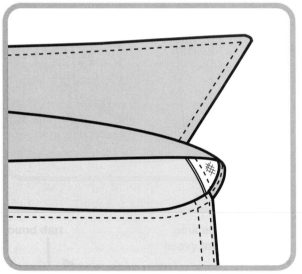

Press the neckline seam toward the collar band.

The decorative stitching on the collar was done after the collar was pressed and before the collar band was attached.

Step 8 – Attach the Collar Band to the Neckline

1 Pin the right side of the under collar band to the right side of the shirt at the front bands. Pin the edge of the front band exactly flush with the seamline of the collar band. Pin the left side of the under collar to the neckline at the left front of the shirt.

2 Pin the collar band to the center back of the shirt. If you cut the collar band to fit the neckline of the shirt, you shouldn't have to put in any more pins. The neckline opening is a bit smaller than the collar band and because the neckline is cut on the bias, the collar band will go on like a dream!

3 Stitch the collar band to the neckline with a ³/₈" seam allowance from end to end.

4 Press the ³/₈" neckline seam allowance toward the collar band. Pin the two end areas at the front bands and any other places you need to secure. You may want to use fusible tape to secure this line.

5 Begin at the center back of the collar band and edgestitch around the entire collar band until you reach the starting point. Press.

Step 9 – Set In the Sleeve

Normally you would sew the cuff and add it to the sleeve now, but if you haven't sewn the pattern before and don't know your exact sleeve length, it makes sense to put the sleeve in first, mark the correct length, and then add the cuff. After you've sewn the pattern and know the right sleeve length, you will probably want to put the cuff on before you put in the sleeve.

Depending on your pattern you may have to ease the sleeve in, or you may be able to start on one side and sew to the other side by finger feeding in the fullness. Sleeves with higher sleeve caps are harder to ease in than sleeves with flatter caps. The flatter the sleeve cap, the larger the fold or drag you will find in the drape of the sleeve. As a rule, for a sleeve that can be finger fed you need approximately 1" more of the sleeve armscye than the shirt armhole seam.

I always put the sleeve side facing up so I can control the amount of fullness and where it feeds into the armhole seam. If your sewing machine doesn't have a differential feed or if you disengage it, the machine will pull in the same amount of fullness evenly throughout the sleeve. The reason there's a cap on the sleeve is so the fullness is at the top, no matter how much there is.

1 If necessary, run a machine basting stitch ¼" from the edge along the top curved edge of the sleeve cap to help ease in the sleeve.

2 Place the sleeve and shirt back right sides together and start stitching at one end of the sleeve with a ⅜" seam allowance.

3 Feed in the fullness with your fingers, holding the sleeve up slightly to help create the curve.

4 Finish the raw edge by serging or zigzagging. If you prefer, you can put the sleeve in using French seams or flat-felled seams. If you choose something other than a simple ⅜" serged seam, be sure to adjust for the size of the seam allowance.

5 Edgestitch, topstitch, or press the sleeve seamline either toward the shirt or toward the sleeve.

6 Baste the entire length of the side seams and the sleeve seams.

7 Try on the shirt and check the fit of the body and sleeve fullness. Sew the sleeve seam and the side seam in one stitching. Finish these seams. Transfer any changes to the pattern.

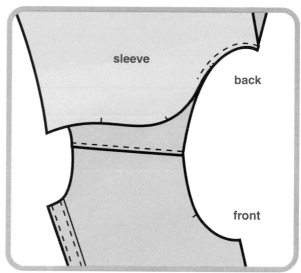

Use your fingers to ease in the fullness along the sleeve cap.

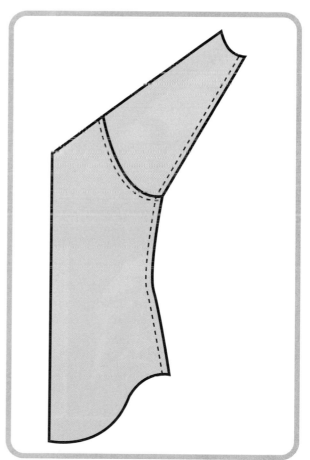

Baste the side seam and the sleeve seam.

Step 10 – Fit the Sleeve Length

1 Pin the cuffs to the bottom of the sleeve and try on the shirt. The ⅜" extension of the under cuff is the seamline.

2 Bend your elbow to make sure you have enough length. If you were unsure about the sleeve length when cutting, hopefully you cut extra length for the sleeve. If your sleeve is too short, you can either make the cuff deeper, wear the sleeve rolled up, make it a short or ¾ length sleeve, or determine how much length you need and cut a new sleeve. If it is too long, cut it off ⅜" below the pin on the seamline of the extension of the under cuff. Adjust the pattern for the next sewing.

Step 11 – Add the Cuff

Depending on your pattern, the cuff may be one or two pieces. The directions below are for a two-piece cuff. If your pattern has a one-piece cuff that folds at the bottom edge instead of having a seam, you won't need to sew the bottom seam or do the understitching.

1 Before sewing the cuffs, put the cuff pattern piece around your wrist and upper hand. Find the finished cuff size and adjust the cuff pattern piece accordingly. Most cuffs finish at about the same width as the circumference of your upper hand. Be sure to allow for the seam allowances and the setback of the buttons and buttonholes.

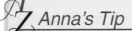

Anna's Tip

The finished cuff (using ⅜" seam allowances) equals the finished cuff measurement plus 1½" (using a standard size shirt button). If your buttons are larger, adjust the cuff measurement.

2 Commercial patterns usually have only one pattern piece for the cuff and instruct you to cut two of that piece. I use the terms "upper" cuff and "under" cuff in these instructions. If desired, pin or stitch fusible interfacing to the wrong side of the upper and under cuff pieces (or to the entire cuff if you have only one piece) ⅛" from the outer edge.

3 Cut the cuff from fabric.

4 Fold and press the ⅜" seam allowance on the top edge of the upper cuff. Topstitch this fold down ¼" from the edge.

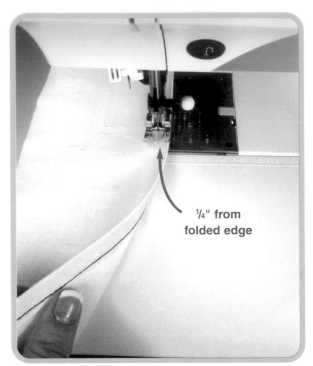

¼" from folded edge

Topstitch the cuff ¼" from the folded edge.

5 *Optional:* Cut the under cuff ⅛" shorter than the upper cuff to allow for the inside curve. (This is the same method you used when making the under collar slightly smaller.) Cutting them the same size works too.

6 With right sides together, stitch the cuff pieces together on the ⅜" seamline around the three outer edges. The under cuff top edge will extend past the upper cuff by ⅜". Trim the corners.

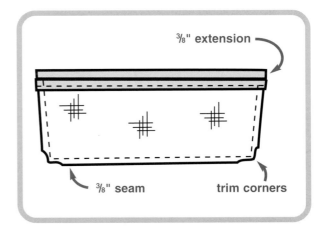

⅜" extension

⅜" seam   **trim corners**

7 Understitch the cuff on the edge of the seam of the under cuff with the seam allowance turned toward the under cuff. Stitch with the cuff right side in.

8 Turn inside out and press, making nicely defined corners.

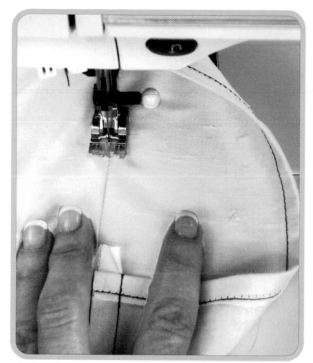

Underststitch the cuff.

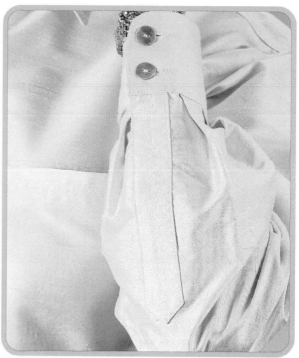

Details make all the difference. The decorative stitching on the sleeve vent and pocket add a professional touch.

Step 12 – Add the Sleeve Vent

There are many variations of vents you can put in a sleeve. The following directions are for a very easy standard vent and for a tailored vent. The tailored sleeve vent is very professional looking and is not hard to do. It lends itself to a bit of decoration on the outside facing if desired.

If the seam allowances on your pattern pieces aren't ⅜", trim them so they are. If you are going to decorate the part of the placket that's on the outside, be sure to reinforce that area with interfacing. I added a decorative stitch in the center of the sleeve vent after cutting the sleeve vent and before sewing it.

Anna's Tip

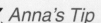

When looking at the sleeve piece with the fabric right side up, the right sleeve has the sleeve vent located to the far right of the sleeve, near the seam. The left sleeve has the vent located to the far left. (I don't want you to make the same mistake I made on my first shirt!)

Standard Sleeve Vent

1 After fitting the sleeve, cut the sleeve vent 3½" deep.

2 On the lengthwise grain, cut two strips of fabric 8" x 1¼" for the plackets (one for each sleeve).

3 Stitch the placket to the sleeve vent with the right side of the placket to the wrong side of the sleeve vent. Start stitching with a ⅛" seam allowance and taper to 1/16" at the top of the cut.

4 Put the needle in the down position, straighten out the sleeve vent, and continue stitching, tapering back to the ⅛" seam allowance at the bottom edge.

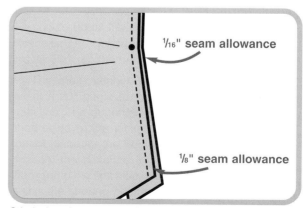

Stitch the sleeve vent placket.

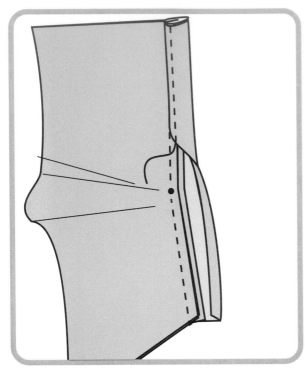

Fold the sleeve vent placket and edgestitch.

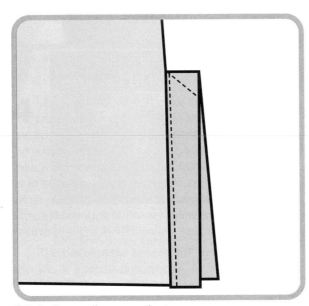

Stitch diagonally across the top.

5 Fold over the outer edge of the placket approximately ⅜" (just past the stitching line) the full length of the vent. Edgestitch.

6 Fold the placket in half, making sure the bottom edges are even. Trim the ends to match if necessary. Stitch diagonally across the folded edge at the top to secure the vent at the top where the seam is the most vulnerable.

Mark the sleeve vent location.

Tailored Sleeve Vent

With these instructions you can make your own fancy sleeve vent even if your pattern doesn't have one. If your pattern does have this type of vent, these instructions may make it easier for you.

If your commercial pattern doesn't have this sleeve vent pattern, you can draw your own vent pattern and follow these instructions. Refer to the photo on page 97 for the dimensions.

1 Mark where the vent will be located by drawing a single line on the wrong side of the sleeve. Don't cut it yet.

2 Reinforce the top of the vent area with fusible tricot on the wrong side of the sleeve. (You will be cutting up to the stitches at the corners and this will give a bit more stability in that area.)

3 On the right side of the sleeve vent facing, mark a single line where the cut line will be located and ⅜" short of the length of the finished vent.

4 Press the outside edges of the sleeve vent under ⅜" to form the point. Also press the other outside edge under ⅜".

5 Place the right side of the vent on the wrong side of the sleeve.

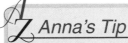

Anna's Tip

When making a tailored sleeve vent, always place the longer side of the vent on the longer side of the sleeve.

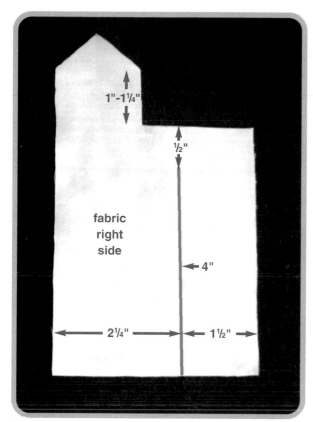

Mark the cut line on the vent facing.

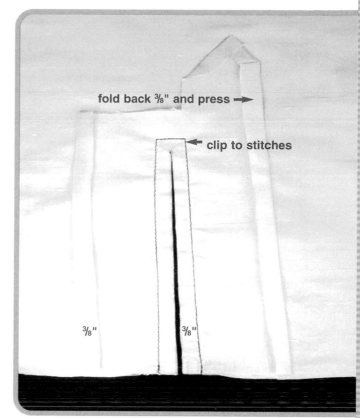

fold back ⅜" and press →

← clip to stitches

⅜"   ⅜"

Sew and clip the sleeve vent.

6 If your pattern has a tailored vent pattern, stitch on the vent seamlines on the pattern piece. When you reach the top of the drawn vent line, make your stitch length shorter. Stitch ⅜" past the line, put the needle in the down position, sew across the top of the vent for ¾", put the needle in the down position, and sew ⅜" down the other side. When you have reached that point, change the stitch back to the regular length and continue sewing a presser foot away from the line to the end of the vent.

7 Cut on the line you drew, stopping ⅜" from the top of the stitch line at the top of the vent. Clip diagonally to the stitches at the corner, being careful not to cut through any stitches. If you don't cut far enough, you will have a pucker, so cut close enough to the stitch until you have a flat facing corner.

8 Turn the facing to the right side. Press the seam on the narrow side toward the facing and fold the facing over the seam allowance with the folded edge over the stitches. Edgestitch this folded pressed edge. (The seam allowance will be hidden in the folds of the facing.)

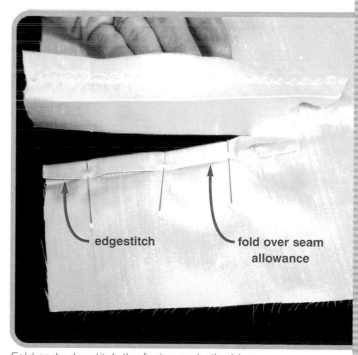

edgestitch   fold over seam allowance

Fold and edgestitch the facing on both sides.

Edgestitch the wider side of the sleeve vent facing.

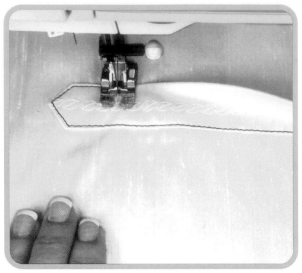

Edgestitch the vent facing across the top edge.

9 Press the seam allowance on the wider vent facing toward the facing. Fold the facing in half to allow the pressed edge to cover the line of stitching, creating the seam.

10 Edgestitch around all the edges of the wider vent facing, starting at the bottom and stitching around the point and down to where the top of the narrow piece ends. Stop stitching, pivot the needle, and stitch back across the vent, catching all the layers including the top of the narrow side.

Step 13 – Attach the Cuff to the Sleeve

1 Stitch the sleeve seam closed about 5" and finish the seam.

2 Fold and pin the pleats in the sleeve. For a standard sleeve vent, turn under the sleeve vent and pin it on the side of the sleeve with the pleats. The remaining side of the vent is not turned under.

3 Pin the right side of the under cuff to the wrong side of the sleeve. Place the cuff on top and the sleeve piece on the bottom. On the right cuff (with the pleats pinned), align the folded under edge of the vent with the seamline of the cuff and pin. Align the other end of the cuff with the folded edge of the vent (left open) and stitch across the cuff on the ³⁄₈" seamline. You may want to adjust the pleats so the cuff fits on the sleeve, especially if you changed the finished cuff circumference.

The tailored sleeve vent and deep cuff create an elegant finish.

Attach the cuff.

4 Repeat Step 3 for the left cuff, but start with the vent side that is not folded under.

5 Fold the seam allowance toward the cuff and press. Lay the folded edge of the upper cuff just above the seamline stitches and edgestitch across the top. (You can use fusible tape to help secure the top edge, but it is usually not necessary.)

Step 14 – Position the Buttons and Buttonholes

Now that you've made a beautiful shirt, you want to be sure to get the buttons in the right place. Don't necessarily follow the button placement on the pattern piece. It's important that a button be placed at the fullest part of your bust line.

1 Decide where you want the bust line button to be located. This is the starting point for measuring where to place the other buttons.

2 Decide how much distance you want between the buttons. The standard distance is 3" to 3½", but this can vary depending on your size. Measure the button placement on a shirt you like and duplicate the spacing.

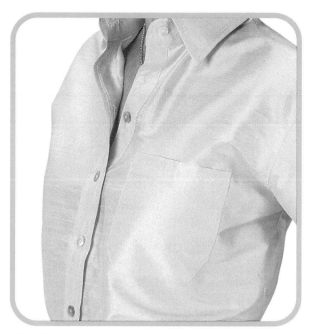

Place the buttons on the fullest part of your bust.

3 From the bust line button, mark the distance between the buttons up and down the front band. Continue measuring and marking until you've marked the placement for all the buttons.

4 Sew the vertical buttonholes, making sure they are the right size for the buttons. The length of the buttonhole should equal the diameter of the button plus one thickness.

5 Sew on the buttons.

Step 15 – Hem the Shirt

1 Button the shirt and make sure the two front bands at the hem of the shirt are the same length. If not, trim them so they are even.

2 Serge the raw edge, turn it up ¼", and stitch the hem, or do a rolled hem.

Western Shirt Variation

Choose a commercial western shirt pattern and adjust it for a perfect fit using the tailoring methods in Chapter 1. A standard shirt pattern without a shoulder yoke and back tucks can be made into a western shirt by simply putting yokes on it.

Design your shirt! Embroider or appliqué the yokes and use contrast piping, yokes, cuffs, collars, or collar bands. Decorate the cuffs or collar. The sky is the limit with western shirts. That is why I loved creating them when I was designing for John Denver. The creative possibilities were endless and he gave me carte blanche when it came to the designs. There are so many options for these shirts!

The embroidery design "Dogwood" is from my Cactus Punch Signature 21 disk, Z'Appliqués.

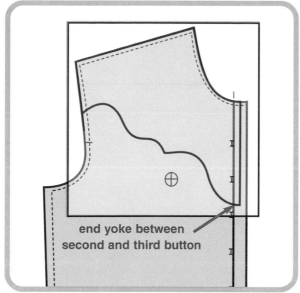

Draw a new yoke shape.

Sew the bias strips together at right angles.

Step 1 – Prepare the Pattern

1 Refer to the directions on pages 86 to 88 for the tailored shirt. The only change is that you should make the under cuff seam ½" deep if you plan to pipe the top edge of the cuff. The cuff will still set on with a ³⁄₈" seam allowance, but you need room to accommodate the piping.

Step 2 – Change the Yoke Shape

1 Using a new piece of pattern paper, trace around the front edges of the shirt on the center line, including the neckline, the shoulder edge, and the armhole (about ⅔ down from the shoulder).

2 Mark where the bust line button will be located. Make the bottom edge of the yoke either above or below that mark. (You don't want a lot of thickness where the button or buttonhole will be.)

3 Draw the shape of the front yoke. Add a ¼" seam allowance to attach the piping or for turning the edge of the yoke under.

4 Repeat Step 1 to make the back yoke pattern piece by using the front yoke as the pattern. Place the center front on the center back pattern piece and trace the shape of the yoke you drew on the front. You may have to stretch the design out a bit because the shirt back is wider than the shirt front.

5 If you want to embellish the yokes, do the embroidery work before you cut the yoke pieces. If you are doing freehand appliqué, that process can be done before or after you cut the yoke pieces.

Step 3 – Make and Attach the Piping

If you can't find pre-made piping in a color you like, you can make your own. I use a ruler and rotary cutter to cut pieces from my chosen fabric.

1 Measure the length of the edges where you plan to put the piping to find the total amount of piping you need. I usually pipe the yokes, the top edge of the cuffs, and the shoulder seamline. You may want to pipe the collar or make smile pockets. (Smile pockets are made exactly like welt pockets, except that they have piping in the welts and are on a curve.)

2 Cut bias strips from your fabric wide enough to go around the circumference of the cording plus two ¼" seam allowances. This is usually around 1¼" wide, depending on the size of the cording. If you find a wider width easier to work with, you can cut the piping strips wider, then trim the seam allowance to ¼" after you've made the piping.

3 With right sides together, sew the bias pieces together at right angles with a ⅛" seam allowance. Press the seams open.

4 Using the zipper foot, wrap the bias strip around the cording and stitch the edge of the cording.

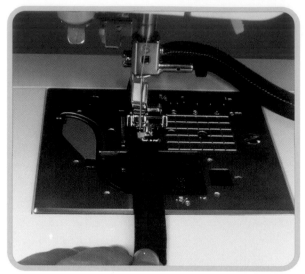

Wrap the fabric strip around the cording and sew.

Press the seam allowance toward the yoke.

To attach the piping to the fabric, sew inside the first stitching line.

5 Before applying the piping to the fabric edge, pull the fabric to stretch out the bias. This will give the piping a nice tight look.

6 Using a regular sewing foot, stitch the piping to the edge of the fabric pieces, laying the seam allowance edge even with the raw edge of the fabric. Sew inside the stitching line you made to wrap the bias strip around the cording.

7 Trim the corners and clip the curved edges. Press the seam allowance toward the yoke.

8 If you are piping the shoulder seam, sew the piping to the back yoke on the ⅜" seamline and press the seam allowance toward the yoke.

The front yoke.

Step 4 – Attach the Yokes

1 Pin the yokes to the shirt front and shirt back, lining up the shoulder and armhole edges. Before stitching the front yokes, make sure the yoke front edge will be covered by the front bands by laying the front bands on the shirt fronts to double-check.

2 Edgestitch the yoke to the shirt or stitch in the ditch between the piping and the yoke fabric.

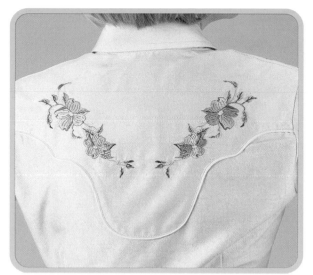

The back yoke.

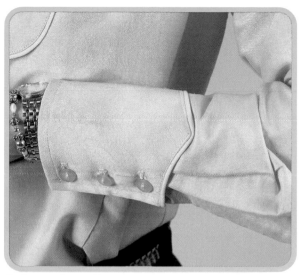

Piping on the cuff.

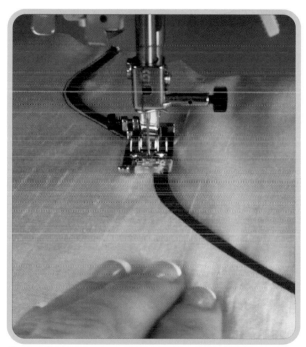

Edgestitch the yoke to the shirt.

3 Refer to Step 3 on pages 87 and 88 to apply the front bands. Before stitching the outside edge of both front bands, trim away as much thickness as possible on the yoke and piping that lays under the front bands.

4 Stitch the shoulder seams. Press the piping and all seam allowances toward the back yoke. Stitch in the ditch or edgestitch the shoulders the same way you did on the yoke fronts and back.

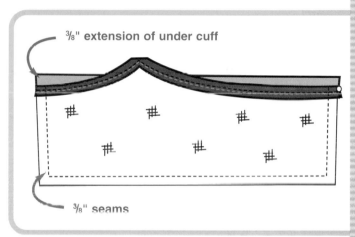

Sew the piped upper cuff to the under cuff.

Step 5 – Pipe the Cuffs

1 Pipe the top edge and press the piping seam allowance and cuff seam allowance toward the cuff.

2 Refer to the instructions on page 94 to sew the cuff. Fold the piping down when attaching the under cuff to the upper cuff.

3 Trim the corners of the cuff.

Tailor a Couture Fused Jacket

The Missing Instructions to a Beautiful Finish

I say "missing" because unfortunately tailoring instructions aren't included in the construction directions for jacket patterns these days. I understand the need to make garments in an efficient way, but there are certain techniques that are absolutely necessary to make a jacket with a couture finish. My approach to sewing has always been to make garment construction efficient, easy, and sensible without sacrificing a professional finish.

My jacket tailoring method is a modification of traditional tailoring, which is all hand done. I have developed a way to tailor jackets and coats that uses fusible interfacing to shape the lapels instead of the time-consuming method of hand stitching. My method is for sewers who have done traditional tailoring but who find it tedious and labor intensive and also for those who have a good background in sewing but haven't tailored a jacket. It includes all the elements you need to make a beautiful jacket – it's more than just fused and sewn as is shown in most pattern instructions (which I don't consider any tailoring at all). You will find that it's not hard or tedious and will produce a very professional, ready-to-wear finish.

This dolman-sleeved jacket is made of raw silk, with one bound buttonhole. The lapels are constructed as described in this chapter, with a variation of the lapel shape. It is quick to make and looks great.

Photo by Mellisa K. Mahoney

This chesterfield style short jacket is fashioned from 100% wool tweed and dark green camel hair on the upper collar, pocket welts, bound buttonholes, and covered buttons. It is fully lined with dark green 100% rayon.

What exactly is the fused method of tailoring a jacket? Tailoring means that special techniques are used in combination with advanced and precise sewing. Fused refers to the use of different types of fusible interfacings to create the shape of the lapels and upper collar as well as to add body, structure, and shape to the entire garment. Fusible interfacings have replaced the interfacings used in traditional hand tailoring. The fusible method of tailoring evolved as fusible interfacings came on the market and ready to wear manufacturers began using them in jackets and other garments.

When I began tailoring professionally, I used the traditional method of shaping the lapels and upper and under collars with hand pad stitching. After many years of doing alterations and opening the linings of many designer jackets, I discovered that the top designers finished the inside of their jackets with fusible interfacings. (You can learn a lot about finishing a garment by looking at the inside of high-end garments.) This method of tailoring appealed to me because my clients were accustomed to this look and it saved me a lot of time in construction. Consequently, I developed my own way of using fusible interfacings to tailor jackets and I was able to create competitively priced couture garments.

This chapter provides the missing details of how to tailor lapels, the upper collar, the finish of the hemline, and the shoulders and sleeves to give the jacket a ready-to-wear look. I explain how and where to use the different types of fusible interfacings. My instructions concentrate on these areas because these instructions are not in the pattern directions. As far as constructing the jacket body, the pattern instructions are fine.

Step 1 – Select the Interfacings

Some jacket pattern instructions tell you to fuse tricot to the entire garment. I agree with this method if the fusible tricot is used to achieve a certain result, but it is not for all fabrics, even if they are lightweight. Fusing an entire garment will dramatically change the drape and weight of the garment. Experiment with fusing a sample piece of your fabric and see if you like the way it changes the hand. Also see how well the fusible adheres to your fabric, as some very tightly woven fabrics won't hold fusible tricot. After you have fused the sample and let it cool, try to separate the two pieces to see if the fusible is bonded to the fabric.

Anna's Tip

Test the interfacings you plan to use by fusing small pieces to the fashion fabric and letting it cool to see how you like the outcome.

There are many fusible interfacings on the market. Depending on the fabric, I may use two or three types of interfacings in a structured jacket. If your fabric is very lightweight or very heavy, experiment to find the ones you like best. I've listed my favorites below. You may not choose any of them but this list gives you an idea of the purpose of interfacing in certain areas.

Fusible knit tricot is sometimes used for the entire garment (if necessary), for the front facing, the upper collar, the sleeve hemlines, and the jacket hemline. Brand names include Fusi-Knit and French Fuse.

Suit Maker Fusible, or a comparable type, is a wonderful interfacing for many types of fabrics. It is a bit heavier than tricot but is very soft and bonds well with most fabrics. Suit Maker can be used to reinforce the front of the jacket, across the back portion, and to add body to the shoulder area for a professional finish. Similar types of fusible interfacings are Textured Weft, Whisper Weft, Armo Weft, or Stacy's Shape Flex. Any relatively soft, medium-weight fusible interfacing will probably work. Again, test the interfacing for feel and bonding after cooling.

Fusible Acro is used to shape and support the jacket front and is often fused to the under collar. It turns out softer than it appears, so don't be afraid to try it. I use it on the jacket fronts of many medium-weight fabrics. Traditional tailoring calls for a canvas interfacing for the jacket front and Fusible Acro evolved from canvas (horsehair). It's available in a nonfusible version as well. If you can't find Fusible Acro, look for a fusible medium-weight horsehair interfacing.

Step 2 – Prepare the Pattern Pieces

1 Cut out the pattern pieces, leaving as much border around them as possible. Press each pattern piece.

2 Refer to Chapter 1 to adjust the pattern pieces to fit you perfectly.

Anna's Tip

Your commercial pattern probably includes one pattern piece for the collar and instructs you to cut two. Make one of the pieces the upper collar and one the under collar. The under collar should be smaller than the upper collar by ⅛" on the outside corners and ³⁄₁₆" along the top edge. This is so the under collar will pull the upper collar in slightly and allow for the turn of the cloth over the under collar.

Step 3 – Define the Roll Line

Note: This step is not necessary if the pattern shows the roll line.

Also referred to as the crease line, the roll line is the fold where the lapels and upper collar turn. If the opening of the jacket is deep, the pattern will usually show a roll line. It's important that you stabilize the roll line since it is on the bias. Depending on the bust line, you might also draw it in a bit with fusible straight tape or twill tape.

1 If you have never made the jacket pattern, either make a muslin from the body pieces or cut the pieces from fashion fabric and do a preliminary fitting. Don't cut out the sleeve pieces yet – you will cut these after fitting the body of the jacket. If you feel good about the fit of the jacket, you can do Steps 2 through 10 with only one jacket front, one jacket back, and one under collar piece.

2 Mark the buttonhole placement on the right jacket front. The roll line begins directly across from the buttonhole on the ⅝" seamline.

3 Mark and baste the front neckline dart if there is one.

Pin the under collar over the back neckline seam by ¼".

4 Baste the shoulder seam.

5 Baste the under collar to the jacket.

6 Fold under the seam allowance on the outer edges of the under collar and lapels. Pin the under collar ¼" past the seamline that joins the jacket back to the under collar. (This is to prevent the seam from showing on the jacket back.)

7 Try on the jacket or put it on a mannequin with the under collar centered at the neckline. Bring the jacket front to the center of your body where the buttonhole is located and put the shoulder pad in place.

8 Mark the fold line with pins on the jacket front and under collar. (This fold will happen naturally on your body or mannequin.) This is the roll line.

9 Pin-fit the body of the jacket and mark any changes on the paper pattern pieces and on any corresponding lining pieces.

10 Disassemble the jacket.

11 Transfer the roll line marks to the pattern pieces for the jacket front and under collar. The pattern will now have a roll line for you to follow the next time you make the jacket and you won't have to go to do this step again.

Mark the roll line with pins.

Step 4 – Make Pattern Pieces for the Interfacing

1 Use the illustration on page 108 and your paper pattern pieces to create new pattern pieces for the interfacing. Don't include seam allowances on the interfacing pattern pieces.

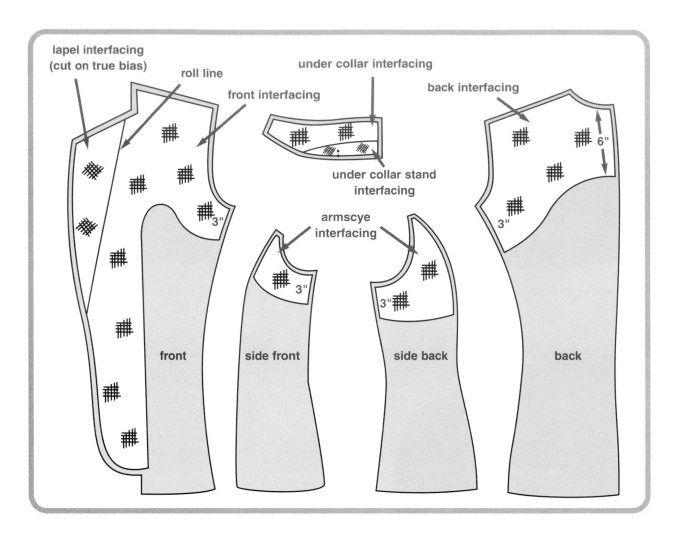

- lapel interfacing (cut on true bias)
- roll line
- front interfacing
- under collar interfacing
- back interfacing
- under collar stand interfacing
- armscye interfacing
- 6"
- 3"
- 3"
- 3"
- 3"

front | side front | side back | back

cut around dart

pink edges of heavy interfacing

Step 5 – Interface the Jacket Pieces

If you fuse the entire jacket with tricot, you may not need any additional interfacing. If you don't fuse the entire jacket, you definitely need to interface some areas.

The sample jacket is made from 100% medium-weight wool with nice body and doesn't need fusible tricot but does require interfacing in the areas detailed below. Unless you are totally confident of the fit, lightly fuse the outer edges of the interfacing at the seamlines. You may need to trim away some of the interfacing if you take in any seams.

1 From Suit Maker (or a comparable fusible), cut the front interfacing piece. Cut around the dart, as shown in the illustration. Follow the manufacturer's instructions to fuse the Suit Maker to the jacket front fabric pieces. **Note:** *If you choose Acro for the front interfacing, pink the edges so there won't be a visible line where the interfacing stops.*

The interfacing will curl.

Press the interfacing and lapel over the edge of the ironing board.

2 From Acro (or a comparable fusible), cut the back interfacing and armscye interfacing pieces. If there's a danger of the interfacing showing through on the outside of the jacket, pink the edges of the interfacing. Fuse it to the jacket back and side front and side back fabric pieces.

3 From Acro (or a comparable fusible), cut the lapel interfacing on the bias and ½" shorter than the length of the roll line. On the ironing board, lap the inside edge of the lapel interfacing over the edge of the front interfacing piece (already fused) by ⅛". Stretch the inside edge to fit over the edge of the front interfacing. This inside edge will want to curve, but pull it in a straight line with the front interfacing. This will cause the interfacing to curl up.

4 Turn the curl down, stretch slightly, and pin the corner of the interfacing to the lapel, meeting the seamline placement. Press over a pressing mitt or over the edge of the ironing board, causing a permanent curl. Let it cool.

Tape the roll line.

Stitch the outside edge of the fusible tape.

7 From Acro (or a comparable fusible), cut the under collar interfacing piece. Fuse it to the under collar fabric piece, pressing the edge of the collar around the edge of the ironing board or a pressing mitt.

8 From Acro (or comparable) cut the under collar stand interfacing piece. Fuse it to the fabric piece, overlapping the under collar interfacing piece.

5 Stretch and pin fusible straight tape or twill tape along the edge of the lapel interfacing (the roll line).

6 Sew the edge closest to the lapel interfacing. If the thread won't show on the right side of the fabric, sew it on the machine. It is important to stitch this line even if you are using fusible straight tape. If the thread will show, stitch it by hand, catching only the interfacing. If you are using twill tape, hand stitch both sides of the tape.

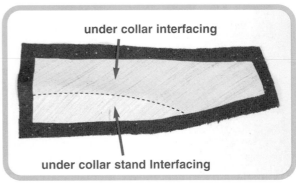

under collar interfacing

under collar stand Interfacing

Fuse interfacing on the under collar and under collar stand.

Use steam to shape the under collar on a tailor's ham.

9 Pin the collar on a tailor's ham and use steam to shape it – never hard press this rolled edge!

10 Lay the jacket front paper pattern on the fabric front and mark the darts, pocket placement, buttonhole placement (for bound buttonholes), center line, and any other details necessary.

Anna's Tip

Cutting the under collar smaller and curling and stretching the interfacing over the edge of the ironing board at the lapel corners are all done to prevent fly-away lapels. The tape defines the roll line, keeps it from stretching, and can pull in the jacket front over a full bust line.

Try using contrasting fabric for the bound buttonholes and covered buttons.

Step 6 – Create Bound Buttonholes

Note: *If you are not making bound buttonholes, skip to Step 7 on page 113.*

A bound buttonhole is a baby welt pocket (with no pocket, of course). Bound buttonholes may seem difficult because they are so small but they make a jacket really special and I can't imagine putting all the work into a jacket and making machine buttonholes. However, time is always a factor. If you want to take the time to make bound buttonholes, here is a method that's as simple and fast as possible.

As you can see from the photos, I did the welt pockets first, then the buttonholes. It makes no difference which you do first.

1 Mark the center line of the jacket with a long machine basting stitch.

2 Choose the buttons. The length of the buttonhole should equal the diameter of the button plus one thickness. The button in the sample is 1" in diameter and $\frac{1}{8}$" thick, so the buttonhole is $1\frac{1}{8}$" long.

3 Find the buttonhole placement line. This line will be at a 90° angle to the center line of the jacket or grain line. The button edge should fall $\frac{3}{8}$" from the finished edge of the jacket when buttoned. To find the correct place for the beginning line of any buttonhole, measure the distance from the button's edge to the shank (or to the first hole of the button) and add $\frac{3}{8}$". The total is the starting point of the buttonhole from the $\frac{5}{8}$" seamline.

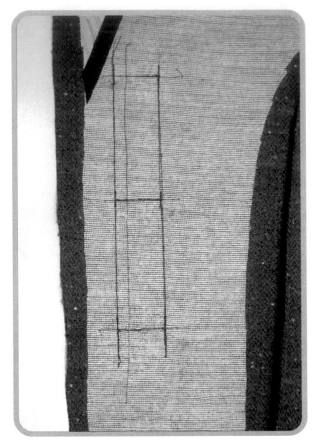

Mark the buttonhole placement lines.

The basted lines show on the fabric side.

4 Use a 2" clear ruler to mark the buttonhole center line by drawing a line on the interfacing side with a fine-tip water-soluble or disappearing pen. (The sample is done in black ink so you can see the line.) With a clear ruler, you can readily see that the lines are parallel to each other and perpendicular to the center line. (Most patterns have good placement for buttonholes. Check to see if the button recommended is the size you want and adjust the buttonhole start line if necessary.)

The button in the sample is 1" in diameter and the shank is ⅜" from the button edge. After adding an additional ⅜", the total is ¾", so the buttonhole starting line will be ¾" from the ⅝" seamline. (Sometimes the marking on the pattern is exactly right.)

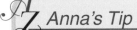 **Anna's Tip**

The larger the button, the farther away the buttonhole should be from the finished edge of the jacket front, to leave room for the button.

5 If you've never done a bound buttonhole, make practice buttonholes on a scrap of the jacket fabric.

6 On the interfacing side of the jacket front, baste three lines in contrasting thread in the following places for each buttonhole. The basted lines will show on the fabric side. You may stitch the entire length of the jacket front or just in the area of the buttonhole.

▪ buttonhole center placement lines
▪ beginning line of the buttonhole
▪ ending line of the buttonhole

7 For ⅛" wide binding on the buttonhole, cut a piece of the binding fabric precisely 1¼" wide by the length of the buttonhole plus ½". Cut this piece on the true bias and back it with fusible tricot.

8 Fold the binding piece in half lengthwise and press it. Place the fold on the line you stitched on the fabric for the buttonhole placement. Pin the binding piece in place and run a basting stitch across the buttonhole placement line, all the way across the binding piece.

9 Baste two more rows of stitching ¼" above and ¼" below, all the way across the binding piece.

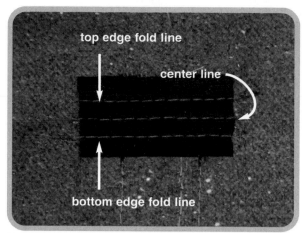

Basting stitches mark the binding fold lines.

Stitch the binding piece for the buttonhole.

The breast pocket (above) is made from the fashion fabric wool, while the welt pocket (below) is bound with the dark green camel hair fabric.

10 Fold under and press the top and bottom edges toward the center.

11 With small stitches, carefully sew from one end of the buttonhole point to the other end of the buttonhole point, ⅛" from the outside folded edge. Most machines have multiple needle positions so for absolute accuracy, line up the edge of the presser foot and position the needle to sew ⅛" from the folded edge. Backstitch both ends. Use a pin to designate the start and stop points, keeping in line with the basting stitches that denote these places. It's easy to see where the stitches should be.

12 Pull out the basting stitches and cut the buttonhole, stopping just short of the ends to form a cut with a "Y" on the end.

13 Cut all the way across the center of the binding piece (the line where the center fold and the buttonhole placement line are located).

14 Turn inside out, press, and stitch across the corners to secure. Hand baste the two binding edges closed.

15 Grade the innermost layer of the ends if necessary.

Step 7 – Sew the Front Pockets, Seams, and Darts

If you are putting in welt pockets, follow my instructions on pages 54 to 56, using the pocket pattern supplied for your jacket. Before you proceed, be sure you are happy with the fit of the jacket front – if you are putting in welt pockets, once you make the cuts in the pocket corners, there is no going back!

1 If you have side fronts that the pockets cross, sew those seams, press them open, and trim to ⅜" in the area of the pocket before making the pockets. If you want welt pockets and your pattern doesn't give

This mauve silk tweed jacket features traditional style lapels with a three-button closure.

instructions for them, see pages 54 to 56. (Use the commercial pocket pattern for the jacket and do all the pocket work from the inside of the jacket.) The pocket may be on an angle, but that doesn't matter. The commercial pattern instructions may be the same as mine but if not, use my instructions – they couldn't be easier or faster.

2 If your pattern has darts that go across the pocket areas and they are more than ½" deep, cut them and press them open.

3 Before stitching the welt pieces in place, trim to ¼" any seams that the welt pocket may cross.

4 Sew the breast pocket (upper welt) piece. Commercial pattern instructions are very good, so follow them. My only advice is to fuse interfacing behind the area on the jacket body where the corners of the pocket will be cut. (The front interfacing should cover this area.)

5 Interface the upper welt pocket on the right side (the side that will face out). On the wool sample jacket, I interfaced the welt piece with Acro.

6 If you are adding pocket flaps, after making and topstitching the flap, trim the seam allowance to ¼" and stitch the flap along the same stitch line as the upper welt. Continue with the welt pocket instructions as if the flap wasn't there.

Step 8 – Tape the Front Edge and Shoulder Seam

1 If you made bound buttonholes, there may be some rippling along the front edge of the jacket in the area of the buttonholes. This is because the area was pulled together slightly when making the buttonholes.

2 Press the jacket front flat and fuse straight tape on the interfacing side along the front edge of the jacket. Continue the straight tape around the curved or squared bottom edge of the jacket, following the front interfacing.

3 Fuse tape to the interfacing side of the lapel edge along the seamline.

4 Fuse tape to the interfacing side of the shoulder just shy of the seam allowance or hand stitch twill tape to the interfacing.

Fuse straight tape to the jacket front on the seamline.

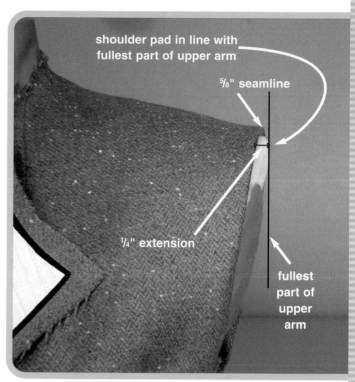

shoulder pad in line with
fullest part of upper arm

⅝" seamline

¼" extension

fullest
part of
upper
arm

The shoulder pad extends ¼" from the ⅝" seamline.

Step 9 – Sew the Body of the Jacket

1 Baste or sew (if you feel confident about the fit) the jacket front to the jacket back at the side seams and shoulder seams. (Do nothing to the under collar at this time.)

2 Press all the seams open and pin the shoulder pads in place.

3 Try on the jacket and check the fit. Pay close attention to the length of the shoulder line. The finished shoulder line (where the edge of the shoulder pad sits) should be in line vertically with the fullest part of the upper arm. The shoulder pad placement should be ¼" to ⅜" past the ⅝" finished shoulder seamline. This extension allows for the padding that will rest in the sleeve head or crown of the sleeve.

4 Mark the sleeve hemline.

5 Transfer any changes of the fit to the pattern and to the lining pieces. If you make any changes to the shoulder width or armhole area, remember that those same changes need to be considered before cutting the sleeve piece(s).

6 Remove the shoulder pads and sew the body of the jacket.

7 Press fusible straight tape (or hand sew twill tape) over the seamline of the entire armscye.

Fuse tape to the lapel.

The fullness in the hem before pressing.

Step 10 – Fuse the Jacket Hem

1 Press the hemline, shrinking any fullness by pressing at a 90° angle. If there's a lot of fullness, you may want to re-stitch the jacket seams, drawing them in beyond the hem. Another way to reduce the fullness is to sponge or wet only the hem and let the moisture shrink the fabric. Consider the type of fabric before sponging. The wool herringbone in the sample is perfect for sponging. The hem should not be over 2" deep.

2 Cut interfacing for the hemline. If you are using Acro, cut bias pieces ½" narrower than the depth of the hem and the length of each section of the hem inside the seamlines. Place the Acro fusible-side-up on the jacket sections and fit it between the seams.

Place Fusible Acro inside the seamlines.

Flip the Acro onto the hem, fusible-side-down, and press the Acro on the hem, shrinking any fullness in the hem. Don't do any tacking at this point unless you don't plan to line the jacket.

Place Acro on the hem to be fused into place.

If you are using fusible tricot or Suit Maker, cut it on the straight of grain. Cut the fusible interfacing twice the depth of the hem plus ¾". The additional ¾" will extend past the hemline when the hem is pressed in place. Fuse to the hem and to the body of the jacket. Press the hem, shrinking any fullness in the hem as you press. To reduce any visible fusing line, pink the edge of the interfacing on the body of the jacket.

Step 11 – Attach the Under Collar

1 With right sides together, match the dots on the under collar to the jacket neckline. Stitch at ⅝".

2 Clip and press the seam open. Grade the seam allowances at the shoulder seams.

Step 12 – Prepare the Front Facing, Upper Collar, and Lining

Depending on the pattern you are using, you can either attach the front facing and upper collar to the jacket and then attach the lining or you can make the lining, connect it to the front facing and upper collar, and then attach the entire piece to the jacket. I sometimes find it easier to attach the facings and upper collar first and then sew the lining to the facing and upper collar. It really makes no difference. If you choose to attach the facing and upper collar before the lining, be sure to leave the seam allowance open at the ends so the lining can be attached. To ensure proper drape, don't set the sleeves in the lining until you've set the sleeves in the jacket. When sewing the lining, leave one side seam open about 12".

1 Press the jacket and flatten any thickness in the seams with a pounding block as necessary. Square the jacket, checking the length of the front, shoulder seam, and side seams at the hemline.

2 Cut and fuse the entire front facing and upper collar with fusible tricot (an excellent fusible for most front facings and upper collars). There are a couple of different weights of fusible tricot so choose the one most suited to your fabric. Be sure not to shrink the front facing or upper collar with the fusible interfacing. (Fusing the fabric before cutting is preferable.) The pattern for the upper collar is slightly larger than the under collar and the front facing is slightly larger than the jacket front. They are cut this way so the underside pulls the outside pieces to the underside, which prevents flyaway lapels.

3 Make a tailor's tuck in the corner of the front facings and the upper collar by folding the corner exactly in half on the bias and taking the pin over the edge of the fold. Come through the fold, grabbing a small amount, and repeat this motion once or twice, ending with the pin in the center of the fold. The thicker the fabric, the deeper the tuck.

4 Pin the upper collar to the neck edge of the facing, starting at the large dots and matching the symbols. Pivot if the upper collar has a corner. Check the pattern instructions for the specific upper collar attachment.

Make a tailor's tuck.

Step 13 – Attach the Upper Collar and Facing

1 With right sides together, pin the upper collar to the under collar, easing in the upper collar if necessary. Pin exactly where the upper collar and lapel intersect, accurately matching the stitches. It's critical to match the stitching on both sides. To help you see the stitch lines, fold the seam allowances down toward the facing, being careful not to catch them when sewing.

2 Start sewing at the center of the upper collar and continue to the corners. When you reach the corner, instead of making a sharp turn, make one stitch across the corner then continue to sew to the pin that marks the exact stopping point. Either tie the ends of the thread or backstitch three stitches for reinforcement.

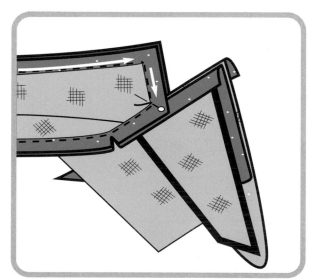

Sew the under collar to the upper collar.

Clip at the roll line.

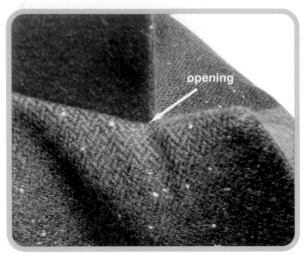

Don't worry if there's a small opening between the upper collar and front facing.

3 Repeat, matching the stitches at the top of the lapels and the front facing, turning the seam allowance toward the upper collar and out of the way. As you sew the jacket front to the facing, stretch the lapel slightly between the top of the lapel and the roll line. Continue to the bottom of the jacket, stopping short of the seam allowance so the lining can be connected, or stopping at the lining, if attached.

4 Trim all the seams along the upper collar and the facing, grading so the longer of the two is on the facing side. Clip the upper collar seams and press them open.

5 Make a clip where the roll line causes the facing to fold.

6 Understitch the facing from the right side of the jacket, stopping ¼" before reaching the roll line and folding the seam in the proper direction. Stitch in the ditch for a few stitches as you cross the center of the clipped area. Continue understitching and press.

7 After finishing this area there may be a tiny opening where all four pieces intersect. Don't try to close this hole, it is fine the way it is. Press the upper collar.

8 When you look at the underside of the facing and the upper collar, you should see a slight border where the upper collar rolls out slightly over the edge of the under collar. There should also be a slight border on the corner of the facing. This is a good thing!

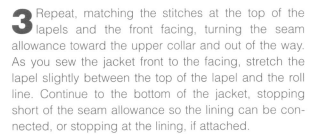

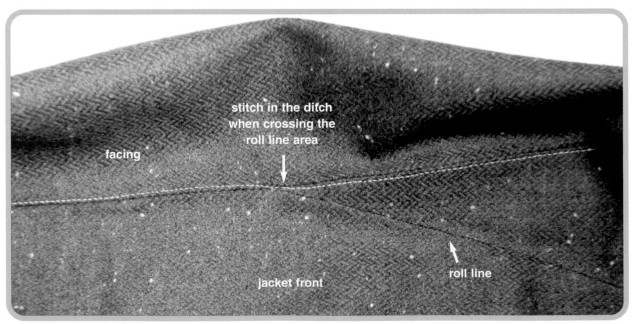

Understitch the front facing.

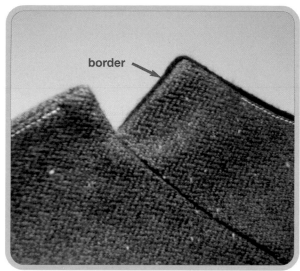

There should be a slight border on the upper collar.

The upper collar and front facing of the lapel should be slightly visible on the underside of the collar and lapel.

9 Finish the buttonhole by basting or pinning around the buttonhole 1" from all the edges of the binding. Cut the facing open within ¼" from the end of the buttonhole, creating a "Y" on either end.

Mark the cutting points.

Stitch around the bound buttonhole.

10 Turn the edges under and hand stitch with a very short stitch. Press.

Step 14 – Set In the Sleeve

1 Measure the armscye on the ⅝" seamline of the jacket. Measure the top sleeve edge, also on the ⅝" seamline. Compare the two measurements. The sleeve should be 1" to 2" larger than the armscye, depending on the style of jacket. If you are working with a lightweight or very tightly woven fabric, you will want to reduce the fullness because it is harder to ease these type of fabrics. If the fabric is loose weave or thicker, it will be easier to ease into the armhole.

2 If you are going to have too much fullness in the sleeve, reduce the sleeve cap by making tucks between the dots on the pattern. Make two tucks on the sleeve front and two tucks on the sleeve back 1" apart. Place the tucks 1½" on either side of the center of the sleeve cap at the top edge. Remember, the deeper the tuck the longer it will be. You can also slash the pattern (in the same places) from the sleeve cap diagonally to the center point level to the sleeve at the underarm. Take out ¼" for each inch needed.

3 Make any necessary alterations to the sleeve piece(s) to match the alterations made on the jacket body after the fitting. Transfer the changes to the sleeve lining also.

4 Cut the sleeve vent. When cutting the sleeve vent, you can cut the shape shown on your pattern or cut it straight to the hem as shown in the photo and follow my instructions. My way is a little faster.

Pin the fullness over your fingers.

Anna's Tip

If you are working with an unruly amount of fullness, you may want to steam the sleeve cap over a pressing mitt or a small ham to reduce the fullness. Don't press down into the sleeve, only the seam allowance. If you still have too much fullness, re-cut the sleeve cap as described on page 119.

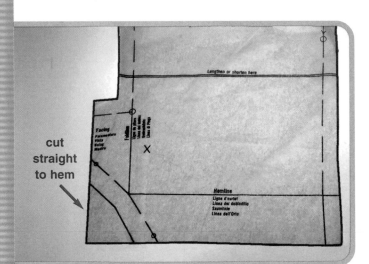

Cut the sleeve vent extension straight to the hem.

5 Baste the sleeve seams.

6 Run two rows of basting between the dots on the pattern piece. Stitch one row on the ½" seamline and one on the ⅜" seamline.

7 Pin the sleeve in the armscye, matching the notches, dots, and center underarm marks. Match the shoulder seam to the top of the sleeve cap. Ease the fullness in at the sleeve cap by pulling the two rows of basting stitches until the fullness is taken up (between the dots).

8 After evenly distributing the fullness, pin the fullness of every tuck while holding the sleeve cap in your fingers, shaping the sleeve cap.

9 Baste the sleeve into the jacket armscye, easing the sleeve cap as you sew. Don't try to put the sleeve on the bottom and expect the machine to pull in

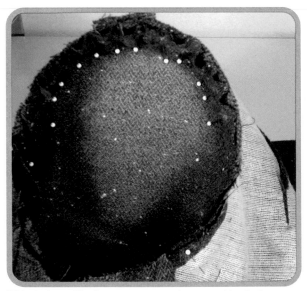

This is how 2" of ease appears in a wool jacket sleeve.

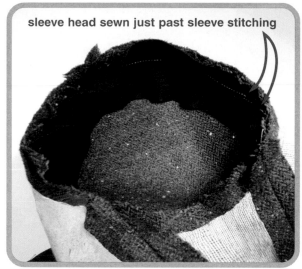

sleeve head sewn just past sleeve stitching

Attach the sleeve head.

Interface the sleeve hem and vent.

the fullness. There is usually too much fullness for this to work. Use your eyes, hands, pins, and the iron to properly ease in the fullness.

10 Pin in the shoulder pads and try on the jacket. Pay special attention to the sleeve and how it hangs on your body. Make sure you have no sleeve drag, which is a diagonal fold across the upper sleeve area. Look to see if the grain of the sleeve is hanging straight, exactly perpendicular to the floor. Rotate the sleeve to hang properly if necessary.

11 When you are happy with the sleeve, remove the shoulder pads and sew the sleeve in the jacket. Steam the sleeve seam with the iron over a ham or pressing mitt. Trim the seam to ⅜".

12 Cut a piece of wool felt, light wool crepe, or muslin 6" to 8" long on the true bias and 2" wide. Angle the edges. This is the sleeve head.

13 Hand or machine stitch the sleeve head, matching just inside the sleeve seam stitching. The longer edge of the padding extends to the sleeve side while the shorter edge is nearest the seam. Sew in the strip so the longer side is also the wider side by ¼". This padding is perfectly graded and gives a smooth look to the sleeve.

Anna's Tip

The sleeve head will set your jacket apart and show that it is professionally finished.

A sleeve that is set in properly lies flat and looks great on the shoulder.

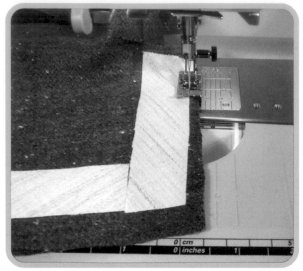

Stitch around the outside edge of the sleeve vent.

Step 15 – Hem the Sleeve

1 Pin the shoulder pad in place, remembering to position it ¼" beyond the sleeve seam as you did in the fitting.

2 Try on the jacket and mark the sleeve length.

3 Using the same interfacing that's on the jacket hem, cut strips on the true bias ½" narrower than the sleeve hem depth and fuse it to the sleeve hem. (Some patterns give you a pattern piece for the cuff interfacing. If you don't have a pattern, fuse the hem of the sleeve first, then the vent extension.)

4 Stitch around the outside edge of the vent and turn up the hem with the vent edges together (or follow the pattern instructions if you want the vent to be open). This way the sleeve length can be changed easily and there is no bulk.

The finished vent and folded in hem.

These buttonholes are cut open just far enough to sink the shank on the covered buttons. This makes them lay very flat and the clean look of the buttonhole is visible. You could also cut the buttonhole open all the way across.

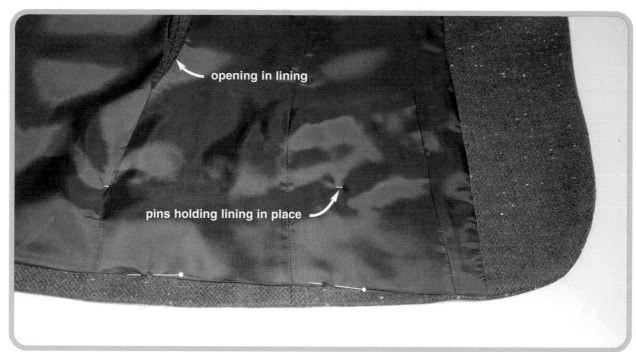

Pin the lining to the jacket.

Step 16 – Attach the Lining to the Jacket

1 Sew together the lining, leaving a 12" opening along a side seam. Attach the lining to the front facing and upper collar (if you have not previously done this). Press the seam toward the lining.

2 With the lining turned right side out, pin the seams of the lining to the matching seams of the jacket to make sure the lining is the same size as the jacket.

Anna's Tip

If the lining is too short, the jacket hem will cup under. If the lining is too long, the hem will curl out. Adjust the lining until you have it exactly right.

3 With the pins still holding the jacket to the lining, turn the lining under so the lining hem is about 1" shorter than the jacket hem. Take out the holding pins.

4 Pin along the hemline of the lining, catching only the jacket hem. Leave in those pins and reach through the opening in the lining to turn the jacket inside out, exposing the front facing edges and the inside hems.

Pull the hem through the opening to connect the lining to the jacket hem.

5 Still leaving the pins in place, stitch the lining to the hemline of the jacket along the top edge.

6 Tack the hemline in place on the seam allowances by hand or with a bar tack. There should be a tuck in the lining of about 1/2" to allow for movement.

The tuck in the hem lining.

7 Make the sleeve lining pieces. (If you used my method for finishing the sleeve vent, when sewing the sleeve lining seam, sew the sleeve vent closed as if it weren't there. If you made an open vent, follow the pattern instructions.)

8 Sew the lining to the sleeve by machine or by hand. (Set in the lining the same way you set in the sleeves of the jacket.) You can either hand stitch the entire sleeve to the body of the jacket lining or machine stitch between the small dots along the lower edge of the armscye and then hand stitch the remainder to the sleeve cap, easing in the fullness. If you sew in the sleeve by hand and want to stitch the lining to the jacket by machine, stitch the lining to the sleeve hem before closing the sleeve cap. You may want to sew the sleeve lining to the sleeve hem by hand.

Step 17 – The Grand Finale

1 Make real or false buttonholes in the sleeve vent.

2 Sew on all the buttons.

3 Steam the lapels and upper collar over a rolled-up cloth or towel for support. *Never* press the lapel flat. Let it cool before removing it from the ironing board to set the lapels and upper collar roll lines.

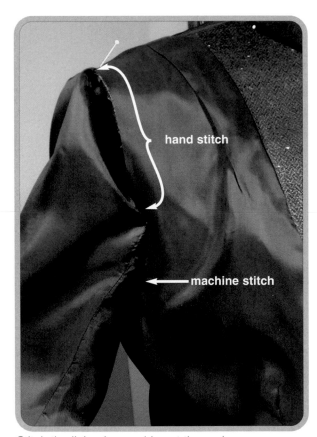
Stitch the lining by machine at the underarm.

$\mathcal{A}$bout the Author

When asked how she learned to sew, Anna Zapp remembers that it seems like she's always known. At age seven she started sewing on her grandmother's machine and by age 13 she was sewing for herself and her classmates, and getting paid for her work. Her career in couture sewing had begun.

Anna attended Memphis State University where she gravitated to sewing, tailoring, draping, and art classes. Her dream was to design and sew for famous people – a dream that came true when she met John Denver at her booth at the Aspen, Colorado Mining Days Fair where she was displaying her one-of-a-kind western shirts. He loved her work and hired her to design all his stage clothes, thus beginning one of the most exciting times of her life. She sewed western shirts, pants, appliquéd satin shirts, tailored suits, and tuxedos for the entertainer, who recommended her to others. Not only did she sew for Denver's wife Annie, his band, his managers, and many of his friends, but her list of clients grew to include Robert Redford, John Travolta, Jacques Cousteau, Willie Nelson, Michael Martin Murphy, and Werner Erhardt. (Robert Redford once asked her to make a jacket from a $3,000 Indian floor rug – which turned out to be one of her most challenging projects.)

John Denver on stage wearing Anna's design.

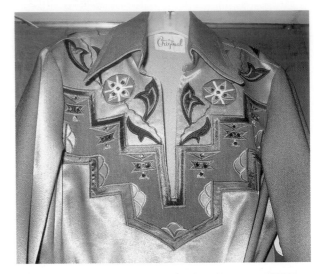

Anna designed and sewed both of these shirts for John Denver. The shirts are pull-overs with tie-belts decorated on both ends. She also made matching pants with the design repeated down the side of each pant leg. She hand cut all the applique pieces and sewed them on with a hand guided machine satin stitch. That year, 1980, she made 13 outfits with American Indian motifs.

In 1976 Anna began to manufacture western shirts and developed successful lines for Neiman Marcus, Macy's, and Broadway Stores. She shipped nationwide and abroad. In 1983, when the "Urban Cowboy" fell off his horse and the cowboy boom was over, Anna returned to her first love – couture sewing. She opened a private studio in Colorado and for the next 15 years designed and sewed custom clothing such as wedding dresses, evening gowns, men's and women's business suits, ski suits, and an occasional costume. Her specialty was making garments from pictures.

A neck injury in 1990 prompted Anna to tilt her sewing machine for comfort and in 1996 she and two partners created the company Sew Ergo, Inc., which produced the Tilt'able and the Sure Foot System, both ergonomic sewing products. After building the company, they sold it in 1999.

Currently Anna sews very special pieces, writes for *Sew News* magazine, teaches, does graphic and embroidery designs, and is working on another sewing invention, "The Iron Genie."

Sewing Garments Easily

USING STEP-BY-STEP INSTRUCTIONS

Lingerie Secrets
Sew a Perfect Fit for Every Body
by Jan Bones
Intimate apparel can and should be comfortable, practical and sexy all at the same time. Discover the secrets for creating great-looking lingerie with a perfect fit. More than 150 photographs, 60+ illustrations and step by step instructions guide home sewers of all levels through selecting, drafting and altering patterns to fit, even for special sizes and special needs. Includes basic garment patterns, tips and techniques for sewing with knit and woven fabrics, and alterations for making specialty items out of basics.

Softcover • 8-1/4 x 10-7/8 • 128 pages
60+ illus. • 200+ color photos
Item# BLIN • $21.95

Bodymapping:
The Step-by-Step Guide to Fitting Real Bodies
by Kathy Illian
Learn to make perfectly-fitting garments through Bodymapping, a streamlined fitting process where you drape a poncho-like length of gingham on the body, pin out excess fabric where needed, and mark the body's landmarks on it. Bodymap base pattern can be converted into 15 different fashion blocks.

Softcover • 8-1/4 x 10-7/8 • 120 pages
170 illus. • 100 color photos
Item# FRB • $19.95

Denim & Chambray With Style
Sewing easy accents for "comfort" clothes
by Mary Mulari
You love denim and chambray and really love the costly designer garments in stores and specialty catalogs. Custom details like special appliqués, vintage linen trims, stenciling, and decorative stitching create the high prices on simple garments. Now you can easily and quickly add these details yourself, with the simple step-by-step instructions from Mary Mulari, best-selling author of Sweatshirts With Style.

Softcover • 8-1/4 x 10-7/8 • 128 pages
100 illus. • 100 color photos
Item# DCWS • $19.95

The Ultimate Serger Answer Guide
Troubleshooting for Any Overlock Brand or Model
by Naomi Baker, Gail Brown and Cindy Kacynski
If a stitch in time saves nine, just think what this book can do for you. Discover the secrets for perfect serging every time. Understand how to avoid mistakes. Close-up color photos show you exactly what's right-and what's wrong-with each stitch.

Softcover • 8-1/4 x 10-7/8 • 96 pages
color throughout
Item# USAG • $16.95

Claire Shaeffer's Fabric Sewing Guide
by Claire Shaeffer
Learn the secrets of selection, wear, care and sewing of all fabrics, including microfibers, stabilizers and interfacings. Content and distinctive properties of each textile are detailed, as are appropriate designs and patterns. Plan and lay out a garment and learn where to obtain equipment and supplies.

Softcover • 8-1/4 x 10-7/8 • 544 pages
24-page color section
Item# FSG • $32.95

Sew Any Fabric
A Quick Reference to Fabrics from A to Z
by Claire Shaeffer, Foreward by Nancy Zieman
Raise the quality of your garment construction. Let your friends think you bought those satin curtains or that velvet bedspread, or share your secret—this quick reference guide for sewing the most common fabrics. Learn what thread to use, proper stitch length, and tension. If you're considering sewing new fabrics, looking for fresh ideas, or just wanting to improve your skills, you'll find this handy, easy-to-use reference is filled with practical and up-to-date information enabling you to acquire confidence, develop new skills, and improve efficiency.

Softcover • 8-1/4 x 10-7/8 • 160 pages
100 color photos, plus 50+ b&w illus.
Item# SAFB • $23.99

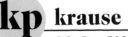